TRAVELING FREELY

TRAV-ELING FREE-LY ESSAYS

ROBERTO CARLOS GARCIA

Curbstone Books / Northwestern University Press
Evanston, Illinois

Curbstone Books
Northwestern University Press
www.nupress.northwestern.edu

Some of the essays in *Traveling Freely* were previously published; the information
shared and statistics cited within each essay are accurate to the moment of original
composition and publication. The author would like to thank the editors of the
periodicals where these pieces first appeared. An extension of this copyright page
appears beginning on page 123.

Printed in the United States of America

10 9 8 7 6 5 4 3 2 1

Library of Congress Cataloging-in-Publication Data

Names: Garcia, Roberto Carlos, 1975– author.
Title: Traveling freely : essays / Roberto Carlos Garcia.
Description: Evanston, Illinois : Curbstone Books/Northwestern University Press,
    2024. | Includes bibliographical references.
Identifiers: LCCN 2024026071 | ISBN 9780810147881 (paperback) | ISBN
    9780810147898 (ebook)
Subjects: LCSH: Essays. | Dominican Americans. | LCGFT: Autobiographies. |
    Essays.
Classification: LCC PS3607.A72515 T73 2024 | DDC 814/.6—dc23/
    eng/20240725
LC record available at https://lccn.loc.gov/2024026071

I'm writing to you today out of sentimental necessity—I have an anguished, painful need to speak to you.

—Fernando Pessoa, *The Book of Disquiet*

We are capable of bearing a great burden, once we discover that the burden is reality and arrive where reality is.

—James Baldwin, *The Fire Next Time*

CONTENTS

THE DIASPORA

black / Maybe

The first friend I made in Elizabeth, New Jersey, was a white kid named Billy. As a New York transplant, my Dominican look wasn't too popular with the Jersey folk. I had an Afro and wore dress pants, a collared shirt, and black leather shoes with little gold buckles. Most of the kids just wanted to know what my thing was. Billy and I couldn't have been more different, but we quickly became close. Even though Billy's parents wouldn't allow him to visit my house, my grandmother would allow me over to his. She took one look at Billy's blond hair and blue eyes, and at his mother's middle-class American manners, and pronounced their household safe.

"Where are you from?" Billy's mother asked, referring to my grandmother's heavy accent. "I thought you were Black." On that day I couldn't have imagined how many times I'd have to answer this question.

"We're Dominican."

A couple of years later, when the neighborhood became predominantly Cuban, African American, and Haitian, Billy and his family moved away. My new best friend was Black, and his mother wouldn't let him over to my house either, on account of us being "Puerto Rican." You can imagine our childish surprise when I returned to my new friend with a similar story. My grandmother didn't want me over to his house because they were Black. We looked each other over. Two skinny, round-headed, chocolate-brown boys, wondering what the hell each other's family was talking about. We looked the same. My grandmother was just as Black as Tyshaun's mother, and I told

her as much every time she chided me about playing with him. What
was I missing? My aunt took me to Black barbershops for shape-ups
and number ones. I spent a lot of time at Marvelous Marvin's, crying
as he picked my tender head before cutting it. Friends called me Del
Monte because my head was so peasy. Yet my grandmother believed
we were something other than what I was living, what I believed
we were: Black people who spoke Spanish. I was living a distorted,
Dominican version of Willie Perdomo's poem "Nigger-Reecan Blues":

> —Hey, Willie. What are you, man? Boricua? Moreno? Que?
>   Are you Black? Puerto Rican?
> —I am.
> —No, silly. You know what I mean: What are you?
> —I am you. You are me. We the same. Can't you feel our veins
>   drinking the same blood?
>
> —But who said you was a Porta-Reecan?
> —Tu no eres Puerto Riqueño, brother.
> —Maybe Indian like Gandhi-Indian?
> —I thought you was a Black man.
> —Is one of your parents white?
> —You sure you ain't a mix of something like Cuban and
>   Chinese?
> —Looks like an Arab brother to me.
> —Naahh, nah, nah . . . You ain't no Porty-Reecan.
> —I keep tellin' y'all: That boy is a Black man with an accent.

As I got older, I began to recognize the differences between African
American culture, Afro-Latinx culture, and being Black in between—
"Black," the giant label America puts on anyone darker than a paper
bag. I also knew the word "Negro" well. I'd heard it my whole life
in Spanish. What you mean when you say the word *Negro* depends
heavily on the modifier, because Latinxs call each other *Negro* all the
time: *Negrito lindo* (Black and pretty), *mi Negro* (my Black friend/
brother), or *maldito Negro* (damned Black guy). One thing remained
steadfast: my family members never identified themselves as Africa
Black, and they never spoke about Dominican culture, or Dominican
history, as having anything to do with Africa. The phrases "Tu no

eres Negro" and "No somos Negro" were repeated over and over by my grand-uncles and my grandmother. They'd use slurs like *cocolo* and *monokiquillo* (basically monkey) when referring to African Americans or other people with strong African features. However, they referred to themselves and to me as *Indio*, a term that means of Indigenous descent. You could say I was more than a little confused growing up, but mostly I was angry. I knew what I saw in the mirror and what I experienced out in the world. Other Latinxs repeatedly called me *cocolo*, and white cops called me "darkie" and "nigger."

I felt like I was living in a perpetual *Twilight Zone* episode. I'm Black, in a country that, by all indications, hates Black people, and I'm descended from people who are Black but pretend not to be Black. Like most teenagers, I was too wrapped up in it to see the bigger picture. There was some serious history behind all of this un-Blackness. And history starts at home.

*

My grandmother, Altagracia Felicia Garcia, was born in Santiago de los Caballeros, Dominican Republic, in 1933. She grew up during the height of Rafael Trujillo's dictatorship. Trujillo ruled the Dominican Republic for over thirty years, and his racism and misogyny knew very few boundaries. Trujillo ordered the deaths of countless Haitians and dark-skinned Dominicans in a Hitler-style quest to "whiten" the Dominican Republic. Snitches kept their ears open for three things: anybody disrespecting Trujillo or his regime, beautiful young girls for Trujillo to rape, and confirmation of Haitian blood in the family tree of Dominicans so they could be ripped out by the roots.

Julia Alvarez's novel *In the Time of the Butterflies* and Junot Díaz's *The Brief Wondrous Life of Oscar Wao* accurately depict snatches of daily life under the regime. Dominicans living in this atmosphere were paranoid, to put it mildly. Some wore makeup to make their complexions appear whiter. Families hid their daughters or married them off, sending them to the mountains or out of the country. People were given to spontaneously praising Trujillo in public so others could hear them.

I imagine my grandmother growing up in that country, staring in the mirror every day, convincing herself she was not Black or Haitian, and probably having to convince others. Maybe she practiced the word *perejil* (parsley), even though she could roll her *r*'s perfectly, just in case she was put to the test. The French Creole accent makes rolling the *r* in the Spanish word for parsley difficult. The *r* comes out like a *th* or, more commonly, an *l* sound. In 1937, when my grandmother was four years old, Trujillo ordered that all the sugarcane plantation workers along the Dominican Republic–Haiti border be given the parsley test, and those who couldn't pronounce the word were murdered in a massacre of thousands of Haitians and dark-skinned Dominicans. Edwidge Danticat's novel *The Farming of Bones* is a powerful and moving dramatization of the massacre, from the perspective of a young Haitian servant girl. Rita Dove also dramatized the Parsley Massacre in her poem "Parsley":

> El General has found his word: *perejil.*
> Who says it, lives. He laughs, teeth shining
> out of the swamp. The cane appears
>
> in our dreams, lashed by wind and streaming.
> And we lie down. For every drop of blood
> there is a parrot imitating spring.
> Out of the swamp the cane appears.

* *

Dominican anti-Blackness goes back even further than Trujillo's thirty-year reign of terror. During the colonial era, Spaniards set up a naming system, *las castas,* that used race to label people. *Casta* means caste. Under las castas, Spaniards stood at the top of the racial hierarchy, possessing all manner of wealth, power, and influence. As Spaniards copulated with the Indigenous and African slave populations (by rape and, less often, by marriage) their children were labeled and placed at various levels within the hierarchy. For example, the child of an African and a Spaniard would be called a *mulato.* The child of an African and a mulato would be called a *sambo.* The child of a Spaniard and an Indigenous person was called a *mestizo,* and on and on. (It is important to note that these are zoological terms, applicable to animals.) To move up in the social hierarchy, one needed to be something else. The African or Negro wanted to pass as mulato, the mulato wanted to pass as Spaniard or Indio, and nobody wanted to be Black. Under las castas, Africans were always at the bottom of the pyramid.

* * *

In 1804, Saint-Domingue (known today as Haiti) became the first colony on Hispaniola to gain its independence, but independence came at a heavy price. The French repeatedly fought to retake the island and ultimately forced the Haitian government to agree to a 150-million-franc indemnity for the loss of lands and goods. The new Haitian government spread the ideal of freedom from slavery and tyranny, aiding South American revolutionary Simón Bolívar in his efforts to free Colombia and Venezuela from the Spaniards.

When the Dominican Republic, then a Spanish colony called Santo Domingo, defeated Spanish colonialists in a revolt in 1821, new leadership sought to unite the island under Haitian rule. For two decades, Haiti and the Dominican Republic were one country, Spanish Haiti, but the economic yoke around Haiti's neck made sustained unification impossible. In 1844, in response to extreme taxation, US and European interference, and rising nationalism, Dominicans rebelled against the Haitians and reestablished the Dominican Republic. You know the old saying: no good deed goes unpunished.

Since that time, Haiti has struggled through various forms of crushing international debt, economic stagnation, and government corruption. During Trujillo's rule, different layers of history, colonialism, racism, massacres, corruption, and Haiti's perpetual economic hardships cemented a hate-hate relationship between the two countries.

* * * *

As a child of Dominican immigrants, I can say that some of my grandmother's people suffer from serious ignorance. A kind of Stockholm syndrome—when a victim who is captured, abused, traumatized, or beaten by a captor begins to sympathize and empathize with that captor—exists within the Dominican Republic. Too many

Dominicans empathize—sympathize, even—with las castas and the legacy of Black hatred Trujillo left in his wake.

In 2013, the Constitutional Court of the Dominican Republic issued a decision that effectively stripped citizenship from thousands of Dominicans born of one or more Haitian parents. The spirit of the judgment seems to have been geared toward deporting illegal Haitian immigrants. However, for many Dominico-Haitians born in rural and poorer urban areas, documentation of births and deaths, as well as ancestral immigration dates and points of entry, is shaky at best.

Poverty and fear of deportation also make it difficult for Dominico-Haitians to prove their status. The situation is exacerbated by mob violence. Dominicans are roaming villages and cities, grabbing Haitians and dark-skinned Dominicans and brutalizing them. There has been at least one confirmed lynching. Bill Fletcher Jr. discussed this issue on his YouTube program *The Global African*, noting that advocates of Dominico-Haitians are concerned because "it appears that the mechanism to identify possible deportees will be based off physical appearance. Specifically, dark-skinned individuals."

I've read articles expressing outrage over the 2013 ruling, which has been dubbed *La Sentencia*. Social media is buzzing with links, videos, and heated conversations. I also know that the United States has been conducting similar deportations. In fact, I'd be willing to wager that the Dominican constitutional court took their cue from the United States. Illegal immigrants and their children—children born and raised in America—are being deported to their parents' countries of origin. Some of these children don't even speak the language of the country they're being sent to, usually Spanish. The US government sends them—US citizens—packing, no questions asked. The *HuffPost* reports that "when a parent is deported, their U.S.-born children sometimes leave with them. But some stay in the U.S. with another parent or family member. Some children end up in U.S. foster care." In 2013, more than 72,000 undocumented immigrants with American-born children were deported.

* * * * *

Here's some hard shit for people, especially Latinxs, to deal with. I love bachata, salsa, merengue, rice, and beans. I grew up watching annual reruns of *Roots*, every episode of *Diff'rent Strokes*, dancing along with Michael Jackson, rapping Public Enemy's lyrics. I rocked a Gumby and a high-top fade when that was the style. None of these loves was or is mutually exclusive of the others. Growing up, I identified with Black culture, arts, music, fashion—everything—because that's what I looked like, what I was: not African American, but Black.

This is not to say that there's some formulaic definition of Blackness, or what Amiri Baraka called "a static cultural essence to blacks." There is not. Neither is Blackness that marketable, sellable product or anger Claudia Rankine criticizes Hennessy Youngman for pushing. She writes in chapter 2 of *Citizen: An American Lyric*:

> On the bridge between this sellable anger and "the artist" resides, at times, an actual anger. Youngman in his video doesn't address this type of anger: the anger built up through experience and the quotidian struggles against dehumanization every brown or black person lives simply because of skin color.

God forbid Blackness should ever be inclusive of Rachel Dolezal. Instead, I think of Aimé Césaire's *négritude*: "the awareness of being black, the simple acknowledgment of a fact which implies the acceptance of it, a taking charge of one's destiny as a black man [person], of one's history and culture." We must take Negritude beyond the borders of literary movements and make "taking charge" part of our very fabric.

In high school I rarely got along with the Dominicans who had just arrived in America. They watched me suspiciously—my slang, my easygoing nature with Black, white, gay, and straight peers. The fact that my best friend was Black, and that the rest of my crew consisted of Cuban, Colombian, Puerto Rican, Filipino, and Ecuadorian friends, was a bone of contention for the new arrivals. Something about the way I carried myself troubled my paisanos, and there was no going back. I was called a fake Dominican on several occasions, and I relished the role of outcast. My motto was "Fuck your racist bullshit. You don't even know your history."

Perhaps they didn't yet understand that America thrusts "Black" or "white" upon you quickly. You must decide; you must know who and what you are. Life in the Dominican Republic had been too culturally ignorant and insular. Meanwhile, in America, some Eurocentric or Castilian Latinxs are passing for white, but too many Afro-Latinxs are self-hating, catching hell, or both while just plain confused about who the hell they are. Most of the Dominicans I know have a discernible African lineage, but too many are quick to claim Latin American status as opposed to Afro-Caribbean identity. Let's be honest: Cuba, Puerto Rico, the Dominican Republic, and Haiti aren't in South or Central America; they're in the Caribbean. We need to reexamine our sociohistorical selves. I completely agree that race is a construct, but identity is a necessity.

I've met a lot of European immigrants in America, and their second-generation offspring. The former come here and assimilate quickly into white culture. The children of the African diaspora, for complex reasons, have some difficulty owning our Blackness. History has a lot to do with it; what our families teach us also has a lot to do with it. We must overcome these factors, educate ourselves, and join the larger conversation—the critical one about how much Black Lives Matter. They're killing us out here, and in places like the Dominican Republic, we're killing each other.

* * * * * *

In his essay "Encounter on the Seine: Black Meets Brown," James Baldwin explores differences between American children of the African diaspora and their colonial cousins. Perhaps the most critical peculiarity Baldwin observes is the African American disconnect from a Black nation, the loss of Black hegemony, and the resulting psychological trauma:

> The African before him has endured privation, injustice, medieval cruelty; but the African has not yet endured the utter alienation of himself from his people and his past . . . and he has not, all his life long, ached for acceptance in a culture which pronounced straight hair and white skin the only acceptable beauty.

Isn't this a derivative of the Haitian-Dominican struggle? Haiti is strongly tethered to its past, to its identity as a nation comprising children from Africa, while the Dominican Republic is trying to be anything but. The Dominican conceptions of identity and beauty and acceptance are rooted in Eurocentric ideals.

My grandmother, our extended family, and the Dominicans I know have taught me that changing hearts and minds is difficult work. It takes time, but it also requires revelatory experiences and forging new memories that help heal the scars caused by old traumas. Unfortunately, Haitians and their Dominican-born children don't have that kind of time. My individual effort at accepting my Blackness and my attempt to build a way forward isn't helping them.

But America and the civil rights movement have taught me that I have options. I can exercise my political power by writing a petition asking the president of the United States to pressure the Dominican government to ensure that the rights of Dominicans born of Haitian descent are protected and that Haitians facing legal deportation are not butchered or beaten in the streets. This petition should demand that our president threaten to cut off aid and issue sanctions if the Dominican Republic does not comply. I can reach out to my local and state representatives and ask them to support the petition. I can use my social media presence and challenge friends, family, and celebrities to put their names behind it.

Just as important: I can tell my story, the truths I've pieced together from history's lies. If you're white, take what you've learned from this essay and put your privilege to work. I don't mean that disrespectfully. And if you're like me—Black, Dominican, American—and you love your Dominican grandmother or mother even though they talk that shit you can't wrap your head around, seek the knowledge and then educate them, whether they like it or not. Start the process of figuring out what the Dominican American experience can demonstrate to island Dominicans about social constructs. Start the conversations that can actively inform the Afro-Latinx experience and the Afro-Caribbean identity. How does the Afro-Latinx and Afro-Caribbean experience in America mirror the African American experience for you? We need to talk about this.

In time, these conversations can help all Dominicans be more like our Haitian brothers and sisters—proud to walk Black and beautiful in the sun.

So, You're Afro-Latinx. Now What?

Congratulations, *mi Negra*! It finally happened. Today, you looked in the mirror and said, "I'm Black. *Soy negra. Vaya.*" You embraced your black or brown skin, your curls and kink. No small feat for a Dominican. You're ready to forego the centuries of Dominican anti-Africanism and embrace your brothers, sisters, and cousins of the African diaspora.

The reality is there is no Black "coming-out party." Soon, it will begin to sink in that everything Black, everything African diaspora, is appropriated, commercialized, monetized, and exploited. Arguably, the term "Afro-Latinx" is suffering from "gimmification." Within our community, there are Afro-Latinxs who claim Blackness when it is convenient, then try and blend right back into anti-Blackness when it is not. The colonial trauma and legacy of self-hate continues to morph in strange ways.

Thankfully, many Afro-Latinxs are sharing their stories. Read this excerpt from Yesenia Montilla's poem "The Day I Realized We Were Black":

> because my godparents were Irish-American
> because I had suppressed my blackness
> because my brother shook me when I told him he was
>   stupid   we were Latino
> because he had missed his Jersey to Port Authority bus
> because he was walking to the nearest train station and lost
>   his way

because he was stopped by the police
because he was hit with a stick
because he was never given the right directions even though
    he begged
because trash was thrown at him from the police cruiser's
    window as he walked
because he was never the same
because we're black
because we're black and I never knew   I was twenty-two

These stories are necessary. We need to shift the focus toward strengthening the intersections of our common African heritage and struggles.

*

Remember: we're not creating a brand. Your identity is not a marketable widget. We do want to move ever closer to a reunification of displaced African people: a political, social, economic, technological, and global reunification. Europeans hoard resources and exact power in the name of whiteness. We need to come together and go a step further by accepting our African heritage and by working to eliminate the "color" construct.

All the new terms flying around are confusing: "Latinegr@," "Blacktino" (my fave), "Latinx," "Afro-Latinx," and "Afro-Caribbean Latinx." You're probably wondering which one applies to you. In his article "Afro-Latinx: Representation Matters," Jose Figueroa defines "Afro-Latinx" this way:

> An Afro-Latinx is a Black person from Latin America. Despite sharing the identity of Latinx, colonial structures of privilege and power thrive within the community . . . Black and Indigenous Latinxs are consistently forced to the sidelines and denied, despite their strong influences to [on] Latinx culture.

Recognizing and accepting your African heritage doesn't mean pretending you're African American. Don't parrot, imitate, appropriate, or otherwise "act" African American. That shit is offensive to the African American community. We are a large Black family, and we're all unique due to our experiences in the diaspora. Embrace the beauty of our differences. You have a Caribbean identity, and because people of the African diaspora share so many traits, you don't need to play roles.

Fact: white supremacists don't care that you speak English, Spanish, French, Creole, Portuguese, etc. Observe what a KKK leader told Univision news anchor Ilia Calderón during a live interview in 2017: "To me you're a nigger. That's it." Language is just another of the master's many tools. The African diaspora speaks more European languages than languages native to the continent of Africa. We embrace the master's languages as if speaking them makes us special. *Coño!* Colonial empire builders believed in the exceptionalism of their cultures and languages. They branded the native languages of the lands they conquered as unfit for instructional purposes; stripping us of our native languages facilitates stripping us of our identities.

* *

Support Afrocentric movements and show up for Black people—Black folks in America (see Black Lives Matter) and across the globe, in Portugal, Brazil, Mexico, France, Germany, South and Central America, and on the continent of Africa. Legal historian Robert J. Cottrol observes in the journal *Grassroots Development*:

> There are significant Afro-American populations throughout the region [South and Central America], although some have been reluctant to acknowledge them. Throughout the 20th century, Argentina, Uruguay, and Chile have insisted that they were white nations with few or no citizens of African descent . . . In the Dominican Republic, people visibly of African descent constitute a majority, but because African ancestry is stigmatized it is commonly denied even when it is obvious. In all of these countries, Afro-Latin activists are changing the national dialogue by insisting that the African and Afro-American contribution to the national culture be recognized.

Many African descendants are now realizing that, in their home nations, they are Black first and citizens second. In his essay "Why It Is Necessary That All Afro-Descendants of Latin America, the Caribbean and North America Know Each Other More," Afro-Cuban history scholar Tomás Fernández Robaina writes:

> It is very important that we recognize how this struggle began long ago, when we did not call ourselves "Negroes," "African-Americans," or "Afro-descendants," as has been used more recently, but as "Cubans," "Mexicans," "Colombians," "Brazilians," identified, rather, as citizens of our respective countries, and as such, rightfully evidenced in our constitutions. Beautiful words, which, in practice, have been mostly lies.

You will not suddenly become the epicenter of knowledge on Black identity and the African diaspora because you read a few articles. Don't pontificate to Afro-Latinxs who don't get it and don't want to get it. Keep discovering the facts for yourself, and if you're fortunate, do it in community with others. Find your truth and be open to listening to other people's stories. Check out Alan Pelaez Lopez's article in *Everyday Feminism*:

> But especially, I thought I couldn't be Latinx, because everywhere I went, I was labeled "African American," "mulatto," "negro," and so on.
>
> But, the reality is that there's no need for me to apologize to my younger self and there's no need for you, my fellow Afro-Latinx sibling, to apologize because there is no manual on how to navigate being both Black and Latinx.
>
> **If you are reading this, I hope you understand that being confused is not your fault, that having questions is okay, and that you're not the first to learn to accept your full Black self and your full Latinx self.**
>
> Let me get something clear: *you are not an impostor!* [Bold and italics in the original.]

***

Visit African countries. I had the European trip fever. I wanted to go to Paris and Madrid, and I have visited London and the Canary Islands. Ultimately, the time away with my family was nice, but the trip didn't bring me closer to my roots. This yearning to visit the master's cities is the same as the urge to learn the colonizer's languages. (*Oh là là!* I speak French, Italian, and German.) European cities are beautiful places, but they're built on the corpses of colonialism. The next international trip I want to take is to Ghana.

Read up. Take courses and workshops. Watch documentaries like Dr. Henry Louis Gates Jr.'s *Black in Latin America* (free on YouTube or PBS). Get your hands on books like Miriam Jiménez Román and Juan Flores's *The Afro-Latin@ Reader: History and Culture in the United States*, Tanya Katerí Hernández's *Racial Innocence: Unmasking Latino Anti-Black Bias and the Struggle for Equality*, Ann Eller's *We Dream Together: Dominican Independence, Haiti, and the Fight for Caribbean Freedom*, Yomaira C. Figueroa-Vázquez's *Decolonizing Diasporas: Radical Mappings of Afro-Atlantic Literature*, Marisel Moreno's *Crossing Waters: Undocumented Migration in Hispanophone Caribbean and Latinx Literature and Art*, Vanessa K. Valdés's *Diasporic Blackness: The Life and Times of Arturo Alfonso Schomburg*, Christina Sharpe's *In the Wake: On Blackness and Being*, Lorgia García Peña's *Translating Blackness: Latinx Colonialities in Global Perspective*, any and all books by Saidiya Hartman, and C. L. R. James's *The Black Jacobins: Toussaint L'Ouverture and the San Domingo Revolution*. As a start.

Visit the Civil Rights Digital Library online so you can understand how the movement became a blueprint for so many marginalized communities in America.

But be wary as fuck too. Your family, the cousins who can pass for white, might not be ready for this new woke version of you. Get ready for an intervention from the *primas* and the *tías*, the *mamis* and the *abuelas*, when you decide to stop relaxing your hair and go natural—"Tu ta loca muchacha el Diablo!"—or when you finally call bullshit on that anti-Blackness you've been hearing your whole life. You are going to be challenged on this newfound Blackness, so hold fast.

And please, whatever you do, don't expect to be welcomed by all Black people simply because, ta-da, you *dique* woke now. Many people of color embrace Blackness when it suits them and then relapse right back into their self-hating and Black-denying ways. Forgive us if we're not ready to grant you a plaque on a building somewhere. Yes, you will get some side-eye, and yes, you must learn to deal with it. Black people from Trinidad to Mississippi have seen the gimmification and appropriation of Blackness ad nauseam, and we're not here for it. Be proud, be aware, and be emotionally intelligent.

I'll end with a cautionary tale about relapses. My man Sammy Sosa meant a lot to me during the 1990s, and especially during the 1998 home run record chase. Here was a paisano representing *pa la gente*, a Dominican who looked like me, shining in the unforgiving American spotlight. After the PED drama and the fall of Sosa and other players, America did what it does best—it forgave its white heroes, Mark McGwire and, ultimately, Ryan Braun. Then they burned Sammy Sosa, Alex Rodriguez, and Barry Bonds at the stake. I don't know how much that influenced Sammy Sosa bleaching his skin white, but damn, Sammy, just damn. It's possible Sosa believed going white would let him back into that spotlight, into the realm of white forgiveness. Listen, I still love him and everything, but don't go out like Sammy Sosa. Don't relapse.

Bueno mi gente: stay woke, stay Black.

Trapped in History

People are trapped in history and history is trapped inside them.

—James Baldwin, "Stranger in the Village"

When I traveled to the Canary Islands, I was reminded that none of the languages I speak are native to me. My flight departed from New York's JFK to Madrid, where it would connect to a shorter flight that would ultimately land in Tenerife, Canary Islands. A few hours into the flight, I asked the flight attendant for two whiskeys. I can never sleep on planes, and since this was a red-eye I figured a couple of drinks might help. I asked for the drinks in Spanish, and his surprise was evident. His expression changed for an instant, almost as if he were questioning the reality of what was happening. A part of me can understand that, but another part of me can't. Part of me thinks he should be used to Latinxs by now, that his experience as a flight attendant dealing with countless passengers from across the Latinx diaspora should have educated him on our differences enough not to be taken off guard by me. Then I got to thinking about language.

I'm American and Latinx. I don't speak English because I'm from England, and my Spanish isn't because I'm from Spain. I speak these languages thanks to a long history of colonialism, or, to be more specific, thanks to being on the losing end of colonialism. I learn in conversation that the flight attendant who poured my whiskey is a Spaniard. Spanish has been his country's national language for centuries and his family's language for generations. When he hears me speak Spanish—a mutt with African, Chinese, and Spanish blood (who appears more African than anything else)—does he consider me a fraud? Does he see me as parroting his language? This poor flight attendant is a fill-in, of course, but you get the picture. What do most Spaniards think about the Spanish speakers in the colonies they lost all those years ago? Do they care? Why should I? Maybe it has something to do with the idea of "talking white." That idiom applies to more than just America's English-speaking socio-ethnic cultural constructions. In the Latinx community, "talking white" in Spanish is trying to sound like a Spaniard.

As a writer I think about language all the time. I'm also more self-conscious about it because I tend to code switch in both English and Spanish. I speak city-streets English, and my natural Spanish accent is from the Dominican Republic. Dominican Spanish is often the butt of jokes due to its loudness, its heavy inflection, and its use of slang. Much like African American vernacular, it plays with signifying and bends the rules of grammar at will. How strange that the consequence of colonization, African diaspora, and *las castas* is that we have a rebellious and beautiful Spanish that fellow Spanish speakers mock. Are we seeking acceptance every time we speak a language used to oppress us—Spanish, English, or French? I can't be sure the word I mean is "acceptance." However, my exchange with the flight attendant demonstrates to me that I feel some type of way about it.

I drank my whiskeys and thought about how, on many levels, we use the language of our former oppressors to oppress each other and ourselves. Invariably the question arises: If I looked European, would I be writing this essay right now? Would my flight attendant have flinched? In my experience, too many Latinxs with European features lean on "talking white" in Spanish. They pass. Aren't we invoking white supremacy when we try to master the master's language?

Some Latinxs participate in an unwritten competition for whose nation speaks the best Spanish. It's typical "colonial mindset" shit, the belief that anything that comes from our colonizers is superior. South Americans criticize Caribbean and Central American Spanish. Meanwhile, Spanish-speaking Caribbeans view criticism from South Americans as elitist and rude. As we chase mastery of the master's language, the master looks down at us as fools.

I should have been thinking about island excursions and new cocktails on the flight. I should have been worrying about how my kids would adapt to the weather, the food, and the cramped living quarters of the Airbnb we'd rented. Five of us would be squeezed into a two-bedroom, one-bathroom apartment that allegedly had air conditioning. The place looked small in the pictures online, and I was scared to think about the reality of it. At home, we're spread out across three floors and have two bathrooms. There's also my propensity for striking up conversations with the locals. This often involves drinks and long hours of solving the world's problems. I like to take leisurely walks up and down streets outside the tourist traps. This would be hard to do, as my wife had planned our Canary Islands vacation from beginning to end. Still, these are the kinds of things I should have been thinking about as we traveled through the clouds.

*

The closer we got to Spain, the more of a curiosity my family and I became to the people around us. In America, my wife and I are sometimes viewed as an interracial couple even though we're both Latinxs. People see my brown skin and her white skin, and that's all they see. When we've been out in public, I've received disapproving looks from African American women and endured smirks from Castilian Latinxs and "white" people. So, this kind of attention wasn't new to me, but on our trip, it felt different—more intense—the farther we traveled. The Europeans I encountered were reluctant to break their stares. To them, we might have belonged to any number of groups labeled "other," groups troubling the European mind these tumultuous days. Perhaps the rainbow coalition that constitutes the Garcia family—my pale wife, my olive-skinned oldest daughter, my high-yellow son, my caramel-skinned youngest, and deep-brown-skinned me—exacerbated their fears: soon, they worried, the entire human race would be a smorgasbord of complexions and nations. By extension, the idea of "whiteness" would be no more. I felt no guilt returning their stares with menacing looks of my own then, and I feel none now as I think back on it.

The staring, the leering, and the danger I felt could also be a result of Europe's rising right-wing fascism. Across Europe, racist right-wing extremist groups have infiltrated government and created political parties. The United Kingdom (the UK Independence Party), Sweden (the Sweden Democrats), Finland (the Finns Party), the Netherlands (the Party for Freedom), Belgium (Vlaams Belang), France (the National Front), Germany (Alternative for Germany), and Italy (Lega Nord) have all seen extreme right-wing political groups surge in recent polls. The new aim of racism in the West is to normalize white supremacy as a political ideal and disguise what it really is, a dangerous and violent form of ignorance. America also caught the virus, electing Donald Trump president in 2016. Trump's most vocal support came from the Ku Klux Klan and other white supremacist groups.

Too many Europeans and their American descendants ("white" people) suffer from a strange cognitive dissonance. In moments of crisis or uncertainty, too many of them revert to their oppressive roots, their oppressive history, and proceed to hate everyone. Racism, fear, anger, guilt, and shame appear to be trapped inside them, and they are trapped inside that history, their history. Extremist leaders know this and carefully craft propaganda to rile people up, and whites fall right into the trap.

This trap works both ways. As the oppressed in this relationship, we have our traditional responses: our protests, our songs, our stories, our actions. Often, we respond with a kind of predictability. We exist outside the Eurocentric, white philosophical construction because we know capitalism is not democracy, and democracy is not necessarily freedom. Not all of us fully accept these ideologies and yet we have limited ways to respond to them. Our response is predicated on white systems of power because that is all Eurocentric institutions understand and because of their propensity for violence. We are also fighting against the racial imaginary, that house of horrors that prevents us from being truly seen by many whites. And still, by the time a new right-wing regime rises, our story has been lost and must be told again. What we are left to question is how much "white" people believe in their own rhetoric of liberty and freedom.

* *

When we arrived at Tenerife South Airport, we were tired and cranky. The entire trip had taken twelve hours, most of it on an overcrowded plane. I was eager to see the Airbnb, shower, and change into fresh clothes. After picking up our luggage, we were questioned by customs. For the first few minutes, the officer struggled to ask me questions in English, even though I addressed him in Spanish. Either he didn't want to believe I spoke Spanish, or he desperately wanted to practice his English. I've had this happen to me in the States: I'll walk into a Latinx place of business, and the proprietor will struggle to speak to me in English after I've clearly demonstrated that I speak Spanish fluently. Sometimes the eyes, the mind, and the mouth refuse to acknowledge what the ears are telling them.

I had high hopes that our cab driver would give us some good reconnaissance on Tenerife. I'm very fond of cab drivers, but we must've picked the worst cabbie in the world. This guy was rude. This dude huffed and puffed on the ride to the apartment. When I asked him about the sunburnt landscape, he ignored me. I wondered at my Spanish. Was I speaking it correctly? Should I have used a different word for landscape? Then it hit me. Maybe he wasn't Spanish speaking. I checked his tag, and sure enough, his name was Spanish. I gave him a good long stare. A few moments later, I felt my wife kick the back of my seat, so I canned the small talk. We arrived at a taxi stop across the street from a small church square. The cab driver couldn't pinpoint the exact address of our destination. He simply motioned for us to walk up a hill. Thankfully, we found our temporary home and then spent the rest of the day on the beach.

Tenerife is like most cities, filled with people from all over the world. I saw countless West African men selling watches, wallets, sunglasses, and large cotton blankets. There were West African women too, toting babies in back slings and offering to braid tourists' hair late into the night. There were restaurants and gift shops owned by Iraqis, Algerians, Cubans, and Brazilians. I walked into a bookstore owned by a German woman who'd lived on Tenerife for eighteen years. More than once I was invited to move to the tiny island. "We need an American. We don't have any here," I was told. These days, the offer is tempting.

The highlight of our stay was a trip to Playa de la Arena, a black-sand beach. Our cab driver, Felipe, was salty and ready to tell us everything about Tenerife. I immediately inquired about the Guanche, the people indigenous to the Canary Islands. Felipe explained that unfortunately, they died out long ago and that *Guanches* now referred to people who'd lived on Tenerife for several generations. He was born and raised on Tenerife and said he remembered a time before tourism, when the island was 90 percent plantain plantations. Felipe's whole family worked on plantations until a shift in economics made tourism the island's primary source of income. While he is somewhat nostalgic for the old days, he appreciates not being beholden to Spanish landowners.

Felipe informed us that Guanches detest *Peninsulares*, or Spanish mainlanders. He said they are petulant, arrogant, and rude. He'd observed Peninsulares who'd come to live on Tenerife give tourists wrong directions, treat them badly, and ignore them. I immediately thought of our first cab driver. Felipe truly delighted in characterizing all the different tourists: Germans, Russians, Italians, and the English. He claimed the English were the best tourists, humble and curious. He was not so kind to the others. It was funny listening to his depictions of German, Russian, and Italian tourists, even though they were stereotypical and rude characterizations. He was like that uncle we dismiss at Thanksgiving but laugh with even though we know he's wrong. Today, I think of Trump. How several white Americans view him as that uncle or that relative who just doesn't think before he talks but seems harmless. Still, there's a world of difference between Felipe and Trump.

* * *

Our last excursion was a trip to a water park. It was a hot day, even though the sky was overcast with Calima, hot, sand-laden winds that blow in from the northern Sahara. I decided to go shirtless and get wet as soon as possible. My wife and I took turns in the water with our youngest. There's no other way for me to say this: I felt like an attraction at a carnival. As I helped my youngest daughter get on waterslides, waited for her to come back down, and gave her encouragement, I was the focus of intense glares. During my time on the island, I learned that most of the employees at local businesses and tourist attractions were Guanches, and we got along just fine. They never stared; they were always friendly. It was the tourists who had what I'll call "eye problems."

I committed to enjoying the day, to walking proudly with my family, my sunburnt skin a brown so rich and dark it sent shockwaves through all those people who leered at me. *Fuck you*, I thought. *Fuck you. I will not be trapped in your history. I will not be the tool you use to remember some bygone era of death and destruction. I will not be the object you return to again and again to prove whatever it is you need to prove to yourself.*

I laughed and smiled a lot that day at the water park. I ran around with my family, getting soaked on all the rides. Trap be damned.

On Junot Díaz and the Literati

I've taught Junot Díaz's short stories and his novel, *The Brief Wondrous Life of Oscar Wao*, for years. His first short story collection, *Drown*, has been a consistent favorite among my students. In class, we examine the short stories through the lenses of various critical theories, chief among them feminist criticism and Marxist criticism. *Drown* readily exemplifies misogyny, double standards, predatory sexual behaviors, and patriarchal authority. When viewed through a Marxist lens, the fact that *Drown* is a reflectionist text, a product of its culture and society, cannot be denied. Díaz is a product of this very same culture; we now have confirmation that he could not escape its pitfalls. Junot Díaz has been accused of forcibly kissing novelist Zinzi Clemmons and of being verbally abusive to writers Carmen Maria Machado and Monica Byrne. Novelist Alisa Valdes wrote that she was punished by Díaz and his literary machine for speaking out about the way Díaz mistreated her. And if social media scuttlebutt is to be believed, these accusations are only the tip of the iceberg.

I'm a Dominican American poet and writer. Before *Drown* and *The Brief Wondrous Life of Oscar Wao*, there weren't too many writers of Dominican descent blowing up the *New York Times* bestseller list. (Although Julia Alvarez's amazing work was in the world, no one at the educational institutions I first attended and then taught at was teaching it. I came to Alvarez's work after reading Díaz. Gotdamn patriarchy.) In America, Dominicans and the Dominican Republic meant a handful of things—baseball, timeshares, and beach resorts— and to Attorney General Jeff Sessions, Dominicans meant nothing

good. Then here comes this smart-ass *plátano* from Jersey writing dialogue from the Dominican diaspora that is so accurate that when you
read it, you feel like you're in your *abuela*'s living room on a Sunday
afternoon. And what's crazy is that the shit gives you all the ugly you
remember from your childhood. To top it off, the writer responsible
for putting Dominican writers on the literary map wins the Pulitzer
Prize for his crazy-ass novel. *Maybe now*, you think, *I'll be thought of
as something other than a baseball player, a jodedor, or a serial cheater.
Maybe now someone might think I'm a writer.* Here was my very own
plátano Picasso, painting masterpieces of the Dominican diaspora.
Or so I thought at the time. I was caught up in the excitement of seeing a part of myself on that stage. The dude was woke. Knew about
Dominican anti-Blackness and anti-Haitianism and was against all
of it. He taught at fucking MIT, yo! I'm like, I can get into academia
for sure now.

   I admit it: I got caught in the lights.

*

My training as a poet demands that I never assume the speaker in
the poem is the poet themselves. I likewise encouraged my students
not to assume that Yunior is Díaz's doppelgänger. However, as a
product of Dominican culture, some part of me always suspected that
although Yunior isn't Díaz's avatar, the apple doesn't fall far from the
fictional tree. The truth is, I know a Papi, a Rafa, a Yunior. So do you.
It doesn't matter if you're Dominican, Colombian, Puerto Rican,
Cuban, whatever. Papi, Rafa, and Yunior are your cousins, brothers,
uncles, fathers, and grandfathers. This reality is what makes people
identify with Díaz's characters and laugh, albeit uncomfortably, at
their life choices and predicaments. Halfway through *This Is How
You Lose Her*, I grew bored with the tropes presented in the collection. I've always felt that Díaz walks a fine line between caricaturizing
Dominican and Latinx culture and presenting us as fully realized
people. Wider success with white audiences sometimes comes from
the white audience being able to find confirmation of certain stereotypes in a nonwhite writer's work. The stories in *This Is How You Lose
Her*, except for "Otravida, Otravez," for me, come dangerously close
to offering this confirmation. Several women writers have noted this

over the years, but because of Díaz's Pulitzer Prize, his status as a
Latinx hero, his one-of-us-ness, nobody listened. We don't listen to
women enough.

We would be foolish to take down yet another famous artist for
being a misogynist and sexual trespasser and not also take down the
institutions that enabled him. Sexism, sexual harassment and assault,
and misogyny have long been staples of the literati: that nebulous
entity that perpetuates literary elitism and tokenism, functioning as a
microcosm of society's ills. Every industry has a version of it. The literati have expanded their reach beyond parties. The literary scene has
evolved to include writers' conferences, retreats, and residencies. The
MFA as an institution is also peculiar in this formula because of the
level of intimacy it promises and, sometimes, delivers. Creative writing students are pushed to be vulnerable, and some writing teachers
even demand it. Predators can see that vulnerability; they capitalize
on it. Many creative writing students have horror stories to tell. For
some mysterious reason, not enough mentors, program directors, and
deans think proactively about these dangers. Not enough of them
advise students to be wary, to demand that visiting writers, professors,
and paid speakers not harass or assault their peers.

I've read at poetry festivals and have been invited to give workshops and speak at universities. Yet, no institution has ever made me
sign a sexual harassment code of conduct acknowledgment form. Nor
has any institution made it mandatory that I sit through thirty minutes (at the very least) of sexual harassment and misconduct training
before engaging with their student population. I can't speak for
everyone everywhere, but this lack of basic prevention seems to be
common practice.

* *

Imagine being an editor at the *New Yorker*, receiving Diaz's submission, reading the admission "I hurt women," getting all those
heart-wrenching details, publishing the piece anyway, and then pay-
ing the author a handsome fee for it. Me? I'm still waiting for the
New Yorker essay that gives voice to the women speaking out about
their experiences with Díaz. Further, their ideas for restorative justice
must be listened to and put into practical action. I'm still waiting

to see what Díaz will do to facilitate healing. Healing cannot take place if we don't look much harder into our mirrors. Teachers, mentors, and advisors within writing organizations and institutions must facilitate this introspection. We cannot continue to pursue entrance to, nor acceptance of, the literary establishment that perpetuates isms and phobias that hurt us. We cannot allow ourselves to become Token because we want that fame, that stage, that money, or that influence—plain and simple. The queer Latinx author Carolina De Robertis posted an important and revelatory thread on Twitter:

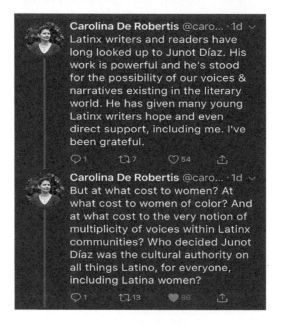

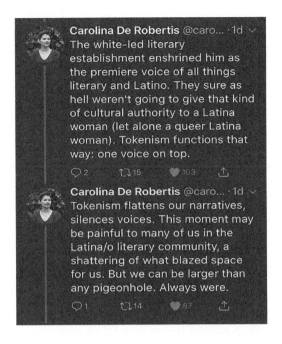

Carolina De Robertis @caro... ·1d ∨
The white-led literary establishment enshrined him as the premiere voice of all things literary and Latino. They sure as hell weren't going to give that kind of cultural authority to a Latina woman (let alone a queer Latina woman). Tokenism functions that way: one voice on top.

♡ 2   ⇄ 15   ♥ 103   ↑

Carolina De Robertis @caro... ·1d ∨
Tokenism flattens our narratives, silences voices. This moment may be painful to many of us in the Latina/o literary community, a shattering of what blazed space for us. But we can be larger than any pigeonhole. Always were.

♡ 1   ⇄ 14   ♥ 67   ↑

My own experiences in publishing have taught me many things. Unless someone has their own press, they can't guarantee me a contract for my book. Some of the poets whose work I admire are not going be great humans to interact with. In fact, I've met a few, and some have been rude, dismissive, and even acted offended that I liked their work. Writers can be fake as fuck. Some pretend to be woke, to be social justice warriors, and on and on. Some writers create a brand for public consumption. As professional writers, we must consider the vulnerability of being a new writer, how a new writer's connection to a text can create a wide-eyed adoration for the author, how a new writer hopes and dreams about publication, the complexities of mental health challenges, and the capitalistic bent of today's writing world. These factors make it difficult to acknowledge that published authors are not always good people. We cannot expect this. It's not normal. But no lie, I'm still low-key heartbroken.

* * *

I met Junot Díaz in person after a talk he gave at Drew University. I took a picture with him. He autographed a paperback of *This Is*

How You Lose Her I bought on the spot just so I'd have something for him to sign. That night, he insisted on only fielding questions from women of color in the audience. Díaz spoke to a teacher and her class. The class was from Union City, New Jersey, Díaz's old stomping grounds. They traveled all the way to Drew, so he gave them his undivided attention. They adored him. I'm reconciling that person with the image of him as a balloon-headed misogynist aggressor who hurt so many women. That day, those high school kids confessed that because of Díaz they like to read now, and I'm reconciling that with their teacher's eventual, no doubt, disappointment. Like me, she assigned his books to her students.

As I look back at that evening, what I'm left wondering is how many victims can be spared if we listen to women. I'm left wondering what might happen if we paired listening to women with protections for women and woman-identifying members of our writing institutions and communities. If we stopped propping up tokenism. If we agreed that talent is not a free pass to transgress.

"I Am the Darker Brother"

On Michèle Stephenson's *Stateless*
and Dominican Racism

Michèle Stephenson's 2020 documentary film *Stateless* follows Dominican lawyer and advocate Rosa Iris Diendomi Álvarez as she defends the rights of Dominicans of Haitian descent against deportation. Diendomi is also the subject of a 2017 short documentary titled *Our Lives in Transit*, produced by Minority Rights Group International. In both films, what can only be called a tragicomedy plays out: the Dominican Republic is shown to be a Black nation plagued by systemic anti-Black racism. The small island nation was once the first Spanish colony in the Americas—and the first colony to import enslaved Africans into the New World. Today, its population is easily 90 percent Afro-descendant. Additionally, it is Haiti's neighbor. Haiti—home of the slave rebellion that led to the first independent Black nation in the West. This might be old history for some, but for more than two hundred thousand Dominicans of Haitian descent left stateless by a 2013 Constitutional Court ruling, a similar struggle for their humanity plays out every single day. In short, the Constitutional Court ruled that Dominican children of irregular migrants born in the Dominican Republic between 1920 and 2010 had never been entitled to Dominican nationality and would be stripped of that nationality. As you watch *Stateless*, it becomes plain that the Dominican government's concern with its countrymen's dark skin color goes hand in hand with its consternation over their immigration status.

The shadow of the 1937 Parsley Massacre looms heavy over the situation. In a conversation with Spelman documentary film professor Anjanette Levert, Stephenson observed that history is a continuum, so we must stay vigilant. Violent threats against Haitian laborers and Dominicans of Haitian descent are made hourly and daily over social media and in veiled threats in the news. Attacks are commonplace and escalating in a way not seen since the Trujillo era. It is apropos, then, that sprinkled into *Stateless*'s narrative is the story of Moraime, a young Haitian girl from Freddy Prestol Castillo's novel *El Masacre se pasa a pie*. The novel demonstrates the ways Dominicans were complicit in the massacre. Moraime attempts to flee by running through sugarcane fields toward Haiti. Her story, paired with Stephenson's ethereal cinematography and double-mirror effects, adds an element of magical realism to the documentary.

In the opening scene, Diendomi narrates the tale for her son: "He [Trujillo] murdered many, including Moraime's mother, because of the color of their skin." It is skin color that foils Diendomi's attempt at securing a valid ID for a young man named Clenol Boni. The official in charge of granting the ID looks disparagingly at Boni's dark complexion. After asking him to state his name, she refuses him, stating she doesn't believe the young man is Dominican because he doesn't speak Spanish correctly. A soldier stands to the side, casting a doubtful look in her direction. Diendomi argues that his documents are in order and that nothing else should matter in a country of laws. She bases her argument on nationality due to birthright. However, the Constitutional Court ruling makes it a moot point. The official refuses them both in a dismissive tone.

The encounter is an example of what lawyer-advocates for stateless Dominicans of Haitian descent face daily. In the Dominican Republic, a valid ID document is a citizen's lifeline. You literally can't do anything without one; attending school, securing health benefits, finding work, accessing public transportation, personal banking, and voting in elections all require a valid ID document (known as a *cédula*). The state is purposely paralyzing its Dominican Haitian citizenry by rejecting, in most cases, perfectly valid documentation presented for the renewal of the vital identification card. Dominican lawyers have termed this a "civil genocide." Currently, the state is offering no options for correcting irregularities in documents like birth certificates and is instead rejecting irregular documents as counterfeit. I asked Diendomi about this process.

RCG: What is the biggest problem you encounter when reviewing citizenship documentation?

RD: The biggest problem so far has been the origin of the parents or grandparents, since, although the proof of the document with which they have lived in DR is provided, the JCE [the Central Electoral Board of the Dominican Republic] always asks for additional documents, and they are subjected to a process of endless research. The JCE ignores that the affected were born in the Dominican Republic and have already proven the fact of birth. This is in the case of those who already have a birth record. The unregistered have no way for their nationality to be recognized, even though they should carry the protection of being born on Dominican soil.

RCG: What causes the problem in documents that have irregularities?

RD: The fact that the Dominican State interprets the status of the parents as in indefinite transit. The Supreme Court ruling states that Haitian migrants have been in transit since 1929. It is contrary to the Constitution and the immigration law in place until 2004, which established that any foreigner who was in the Dominican Republic for more than ten days could be in another immigration status, but not in transit. The Constitution only indicates two exceptions to acquiring nationality:

> People born in the national territory, with the exception of the sons and daughters of foreign members of diplomatic and consular legations, of foreigners that find themselves in transit or reside illegally in Dominican territory. All foreigners are considered people in transit as defined in Dominican laws.

> However, Haitian migrants came to the Dominican Republic to work in the sugarcane fields, and in most cases, they were taken in by the state or private

companies. The *zafra*, which is the sugar production period, had a duration of six to eight months. The state or the company provided the workers with a document called a *ficha*; the workers used it to collect their pay every week or fortnight. The companies used it to deduct funds for health insurance, social security, and other taxes (although today the state does not want to pay workers their pensions), and with that same document they went to officials to register their children. And the authorities accepted the ficha as a complete and valid form of identification. Now, the state alleges the irregularity of their documents based on the status of the parents. By invoking the transit rule from 1929–2013, they invalidate the ficha and every other document, a fact that violates the Constitution, even the new Constitution of 2010. No law can be above the Constitution or international treaties.

RCG: What excuse or reason does the government provide for rejecting the documents?

RD: The fact that an irregular document cannot generate rights, referring to the supposed state of transit of the parents. Applicants carry the stigma that when they submit an application with a French last name, they will receive different treatment. Applicants are also asked questions that are nothing more than delaying tactics in the process.

*

Diendomi is personally familiar with the Dominican Haitian experience. Both her parents were Haitian laborers in the *bateyes*, Dominican sugarcane plantations. It was a hard life. She explains that during zafra, food is plentiful for workers and their families. However, after the six-month harvest period is over, workers eat once a day, usually in the evening. The crux of Diendomi's advocacy involves visiting bateyes and ensuring that community members have the necessary paperwork to avoid further disenfranchisement, harassment, and deportation.

Stateless cuts to former President Danilo Medina explaining the National Regularization Plan. Medina denounces the international community for criticizing the plan and its impact on Dominicans of Haitian descent. He denies the fact that two hundred thousand Dominicans have been left stateless. Stephenson has purposefully pixelated and blown up the footage of politicians. The effect is that the propagandistic tone of the speeches is rendered tactile. Meanwhile, Diendomi's colleague, Genaro Rincón, is beaten savagely by a crowd of anti-Haitian nationalists. On a television program called *A Partir de Ahora*, Rincón explains that he was stoned with chunks of cinder blocks and stomped on. He presents his injuries to the camera. A guest on the same program, Diendomi decries the violence and rebukes the government for its silence in the face of increasing threats and attacks.

* *

When Gladys Feliz-Pimentel first appears in the film, she is in Dajabón, at the Dominican Republic–Haiti border, taking photographs and being a nuisance. In many ways, she's reminiscent of a Trump supporter or an American "Karen." Feliz-Pimentel observes, "Damn, they can cross to our side [of the border] so easily, and we can't enter [their side]." A soldier informs her that the Haitians entering and leaving are licensed merchants who cross the border daily to conduct business. She is not convinced. "I can't cross from there [the border gate into Haiti], but they can come here [the Dominican Republic] whenever they want." Feliz-Pimentel is a member of the Dominican nationalist movement. Its rhetoric is eerily like that of right-wing groups around the globe and in America in particular. The movement is anti-Haitian, anti-immigrant, and racist, wrapping all of these destructive beliefs into the national flag. Feliz-Pimentel accuses Haitians of assaults, rapes, and stabbings. Sound familiar? It should: Donald Trump ran for president using similar racist rhetoric as his platform.

Feliz-Pimentel claims her lineage goes all the way back to El Grito de Capotillo, the 1863 rebellion against Spain. She claims her ancestor fought alongside Haitians (the Dominican Republic and Haiti fought side by side to defeat Spain) and was even president during the transition period. She claims she's not racist. She simply believes that

Haitians belong in Haiti, explaining on camera that "Haitians have always fought by our side. Including in 1965 against the gringos. We have always lived in fraternity. Them in their country and us in ours. Except when they've come here and tried to steal our country." The rhetoric is eerily reminiscent of American racist xenophobia. I asked Diendomi about her understanding of the nationalist movement. I wanted to understand if the nationalists are supportive of the Trujillo dictatorship and its policies.

> RCG: Is the nationalist movement automatically supportive of the Trujillo regime, or do they distance themselves from him?
>
> RD: Interesting question. If we take into account the nationalist movement's speeches and organizational behaviors, you could say that they are Trujillistas. They've publicly stated many times that the state should repeat what Trujillo did. I hear them say that they are not racists, but they also say they want nothing to do with Haitians. Their constant contempt for our African heritage and their cult of Eurocentrism leads me to understand that they are Trujillistas.

* * *

The film cuts to former President Medina questioning how the Dominican Republic can be considered a racist nation when 80 percent of its population is Black and mulatto. In a classic example of talking out of both sides of one's mouth, he asks, "How can Dominicans be accused of being racist toward Haitians when they live and coexist with us everywhere in our country?" In the documentary *Our Lives in Transit*, the same clip shows Medina stating publicly:

> Today 13 percent of women having babies in Dominican hospitals are Haitian . . . Not only Haitian women that are residents in the Dominican Republic, but also women who cross the border to give birth here because it is cheaper than in Haiti, where they have to pay . . . They are undocumented, but they walk the streets of the Dominican Republic freely,

without any police or any immigration stopping them to ask if they have a passport or a visa to reside in the Dominican Republic.

This rhetoric is an exhortation to the public to accost and harass "suspected" illegal Haitians. Many advocates blame the wave of anti-Haitian violence on this type of state-sponsored rhetoric. At this point in the film, Moraime's narrative has her running for her life through the cane fields on the night of the Parsley Massacre.

* * * *

As the film progresses, Diendomi tries to help her cousin, Juan Teofilo, straighten out his documentation and return to the Dominican Republic. Juan Teofilo decided to move to Haiti after *La Sentencia* rather than be deported. Diendomi visits him in Haiti, her first-ever trip to her forefather's land, and the trip fills her with pride and joy. Juan Teofilo is a wonderfully proud man and a devoted father who has been stripped of his identity, his homeland, and his relationship with his Dominican-born children by the ruling. He is understandably bitter, and Diendomi spends most of their time reassuring him of the need to remain steadfast. After securing an interview to review his documentation and hopefully resolve his situation, the pair undertakes the perilous journey of getting Juan Teofilo from the Haitian border to the JCE in Santo Domingo. Diendomi recounts a story in which a group of Dominicans of Haitian descent was attacked on a public bus. She states that, during the altercation, the conductor announced, "The ruling has spoken; you are not Dominican."

While awaiting his appointment, Juan Teofilo visits his children, which is easily one of the most heartbreaking scenes in the film. At the appointment, he is told there is a discrepancy between his mother's age listed on her death certificate and the birthdate on her birth certificate. Due to this discrepancy, the interviewer declares Juan Teofilo's paperwork counterfeit. The interviewer effectively ends the interview by taking out his cell phone and flipping through his social media. The state makes no effort to correct and validate the documentation of Dominicans of Haitian descent.

RCG: What are the main challenges that Dominicans of Haitian descent face in locating these necessary documents?

RD: The main challenge is the political will of the authorities. From there, other challenges emerge. We always have to think of the situation as two affected groups: First, those who have already been registered. Their challenge includes whether or not the parents can find the documents with which they were registered. In many cases, due to atmospheric phenomena, fires, or the parents' death, they cannot present the documents. If you have financial resources, you can go to Santo Domingo (the capital) to the main headquarters of the JCE so that you can interview with the inspectorial department, and this is in addition to being able to find each means of proof that the government requires. You must also be able to secure legal representation when the JCE demands nullity before the ordinary courts (so as not to be left in a defenseless state). All of this costs money. There's also a question of the will of the JCE and its officials to get the situation resolved.

Second, some have never been registered. In the case of mixed couples (Haitian mother or of Haitian descent with Dominican father), if the mother does not have a document (Dominican ID or legal residence), even if the father is Dominican, the child is registered as a foreigner, leaving [the child] in a legal limbo in which they do not recognize the child's nationality.

RCG: Do other Dominicans, not of Haitian descent, have similar problems?

RD: No, they don't have similar problems. Even though we have a problem with their registrations in the country, which in many cases are generational, from my experience, they have a different and more agile course of action to rectify their situation.

* * * * *

Another cut to Medina. In this scene, he is refuting claims that two hundred thousand Dominicans of Haitian descent have been left stateless: "In the Dominican Republic, the number of stateless people is zero. Of course, we sometimes make mistakes. If this happens, and someone presents their case to our government, have no doubt that we will find the solution. But until now, that has not happened." Juan Teofilo and countless others serve as proof that Medina and the state are lying.

* * * * * *

When next we see Feliz-Pimentel, she is attending what might be mistaken for a meeting of harmless aunties and grandmothers. Nothing could be further from the truth. The women are members of the nationalist movement, and they spout timeworn racist tropes about Black criminality, sexual malevolence and deviance, and propensity for violence. These same myths still plague the United States. In her book *The Borders of Dominicanidad: Race, Nation, and Archives of Contradiction*, Dr. Lorgia García-Peña writes, "During the early years of the foundation of the Dominican Republic (1844–65), the United States supported the idea of Dominican racial superiority over Haiti and disavowed Haiti as racially inferior and thus unfit for self-government." It is no wonder, then, that the nationalists sound like American racists and right-wing ideologues.

Feliz-Pimentel claims, "Women make up 90 percent of our nationalist movement. Women, 90 percent. But those men who are the 10 percent are hotheaded. They want to fight." The nationalists refer to the Haitians as "the Haitian problem," and they use words like "invasion" when discussing Haitian immigration. In many places, anti-Haitian graffiti is spray-painted on walls. The nationalists openly claim that Haiti plans to "dump all Haitian citizens on Dominican soil." The rhetoric at nationalist rallies carries over to social media, where it combines with violent threats that lead to realized violence on both city streets and in rural communities. The camera cuts to a nationalist rally that mirrors extremist nationalist rallies globally. There is always the vilified other (refugees, immigrants, Muslims, etc.) who must be ousted or defeated, and always rage and violence.

At the heart of this violence and vitriol is the nationalist's desperate need to completely disavow Africa and African lineage. Blackness and Africanness are viewed as distinctly negative. Dominicans of Haitian descent are acutely aware that racism and colorism are the main causes of their daily dehumanization. Diendomi seeks political solutions to these problems. She believes that through the people's sociopolitical actions, and with international pressure, it is possible to force the state to capitulate. To that end, when she is asked to run for congress, she accepts. Her campaign gets off to a positive start, though her funds are limited, but it soon becomes apparent that the people are cynical about long-term political change. They are more interested in the short-term bribes that proliferate on election day. Political candidates offer voters one hundred Dominican pesos ($1.75 USD) for their vote.

Diendomi asks the people to think beyond the bribe and to think about the future. I wanted to understand the machine behind the bribes.

> RCG: Who finances the bribes that are given to voters?
>
> RD: The political party's candidates. The bigger question we need answered is "Who finances the political parties?"
>
> RCG: What is the mechanism to get beyond the one-hundred-peso bribe?
>
> RD: On many occasions, the promises of jobs or improvements to the community, which are never kept, lead to voters trying to monopolize what they can get on election day. The voters know they will not see that candidate again. This has been the case historically. Traditional politicians always identify a leader who can convince the voters to accept the bribe. When the voter refuses, threats are sometimes used.

The election scenes in the documentary capture the Dominican people's struggle. Either they sacrifice the immediate meal, beverage, cell phone, or utility service they could consume with the one hundred pesos, or they potentially risk their lives by refusing to pay the bribe. Lurking somewhere within this corrupt political ether is the far-off chance that a political candidate will improve their situation.

RCG: How can Dominican Americans and our allies help Dominicans?

RD: First, by understanding that nationality and statelessness in the Dominican Republic have not yet been resolved. We can still affect change by holding events and mobilizations that summon the Dominican state to take up the issue. Additionally, by supporting local organizations like the Recognized Movement (reconoci.do), whose greatest limitation is the lack of economic resources for field work. The Recognized Movement is an NGO working towards the recognition of Dominicans of Haitian descent as full citizens. Also, by continuing to empower local leadership. Finally, by sending letters to embassies.

* * * * * * *

How do you explain to a nation's populace who they actually are, and the shared history they are part of? Where in the long and painful process do you begin? With the transatlantic slave trade? Colonialism and postcolonialism? Dictatorships? The global Black Power movement? Pan-Africanism? What drives a nation of Black people to see themselves not only as the victims of past colonial horrors but also as its beneficiaries? Scholars have written countless books to explain the complexities of Dominican identity. These books examine history, language, and even the so-called unique relationship that existed on the island between slave and slave-master. At the end of the day, Dominicans must be able to look at their darker-skinned brothers and sisters and see a human being worthy of love and respect, but for too long, this has proved difficult for many. Until that embrace happens in a meaningful and lasting way, one that tips the scales of justice toward equity for Dominicans of Haitian descent, scholars can write all the books they want.

Toward the end of *Stateless*, the camera shows us a billboard that reads NO NATION WITHOUT BORDERS. THE WALL. BORDER CONTROL. Again, it is all too familiar. Moraime's parallel narrative ends tragically. She is close to escaping the massacre when a hungry dog's barking gives her location away and soldiers discover her. Diendomi narrates, "Soldiers drunk on rum and blood don't forgive. Moraime's body floated on the river. And the night fell silent."

THIS IS AMERICA

Ten Minutes of Terror

They wanted to be confirmed in something
by you. By your face, by your terror of them.

—James Baldwin, "The Last Interview"

There's a running joke between BIPOC faculty and students on my campus that the boulevard leading into the college is a training facility for police stops—training for both the police officers conducting the stops and for the people of color they pull over. The rule is you drive like a turtle, your hands at ten and two o'clock, and you stay casual, whatever that means. But Black people and people of color already know this unwritten rule; I'm not saying anything new here. I've driven the boulevard countless times over the years as a student on my way to the college, and more recently as a faculty member on my way to work. I've been lucky not to be pulled over, until today.

*

I stopped at the intersection. A sheriff coming from the right side of the intersecting street made a left and stared intently at me and my car. We made eye contact, or a better way to describe it would be face-to-face contact. He was wearing pitch-black wraparound sunglasses and a ball cap pulled down low. After he drove past, I looked in my rearview and sideview mirrors and watched him continue down the

road. I drove on, my mind running through possible scenarios: Will
he make a U-turn and come at me full speed? Is he calling in other
cars to cut me off up ahead? Should I speed up and put as much distance between us as possible? I played it casual and kept driving at a
slower-than-usual speed, but inevitably all those videos ran through
my head. You know the ones I'm talking about. I fell into a daydream
of myself starring in an episode of the American theater of death
porn—the destruction of the Black body. Then I saw the sheriff's jeep
behind the car directly behind me. I needed to focus. I went into my
glove compartment and pulled out the cheap vinyl pouch with my
registration and insurance card in it. I took out my driver's license
too, and placed all of it in the visor in front of me.

The sheriff switched lanes but didn't pass me. He stayed in my
blind spot. The car behind me turned down a side street, and the
sheriff got behind me. At this point, I figured he was running my
plates. He stayed behind me for a while. To be precise, he stayed there
through two traffic lights, two blocks apart. He switched lanes and
returned to my blind spot. Another car got behind me, and after a
few minutes he cut that car off, got in close behind me, flashed his
lights, and pulled me over. *Took you long enough*, I thought.

This is how terror works. Everyday moments become loaded with
the fear of being maimed or killed, or the fear of losing a loved one.
The flood of cell phone videos depicting police violence, much like
the news stories of ISIS attacks in Europe and mass shootings in
America, keep us in a state of fear. This fear is multiplied exponen-
tially into something else when the state, presumably charged with
our safety, does nothing. And as these events accumulate and the
world's citizens receive no justice or resolution, we are all left adrift
and in terror. We begin to distrust police, politicians, the courts,
the laws—the whole system. I think of this passage from George
Orwell's *1984*:

> But always—do not forget this, Winston—always there
> will be the intoxication of power, constantly increasing and
> constantly growing subtler. Always, at every moment, there
> will be the thrill of victory, the sensation of trampling on an
> enemy who is helpless. If you want a picture of the future,
> imagine a boot stamping on a human face—forever.

* *

Critics of police reform, those people James Baldwin called "the vast heedless, unthinking, cruel white majority," dismiss what I'm about to say. They can argue it all day if they want to, but the truth is that for Black people and other people of color, looking in the sideview mirror as a police officer approaches their car is terror only other BIPOC can understand. I watched the sheriff approach my car, his hand on his gun, and I watched him watch me watch him. I thought about power, but mostly I was thankful my children weren't with me. I am convinced that the terror the state wants us to feel, that the law enforcement officers who summarily execute BIPOC in this country want us to feel, that the Klan and their affiliates (many of whom have infiltrated state and law enforcement agencies) want us to feel, is the same terror they harbor of *us* inside the nebulous psyche of whiteness. These are the moments when Zora Neale Hurston's words, restated in Claudia Rankine's *Citizen: An American Lyric*, haunt me the most: "I feel most colored when I am thrown against a sharp white background."

I lowered my window and said nothing. I waited for the sheriff to speak. He raised his hand and pointed to my inspection sticker. "I thought your sticker was a rejection tag from inspection," he said. "I see now it's orange and is still active. You're okay. You can go." And I said thank you. Never mind that my inspection sticker is yellow. He was courteous, he walked back to his jeep, and he drove off.

Maybe you think this is the part where I say, "You see, not all cops are bad" or some other comforting nonsense. All I knew that day was that I sat in my car alone. That if he had shot me dead, there would have been no witness. In the hands of the state, BIPOC live in the void. I'd needed to place all my trust—my very life—in the hands of an armed agent of the state. Meanwhile, there is irrefutable evidence that if he'd wanted to kill me, he could have. The state would have done nothing about it.

The most unforgivable aspect of police violence is the wall of silence. Think about the officers who stood by as their fellow officer kneeled on George Floyd's neck, ultimately murdering Floyd. Think of the second officer in the dashcam video of Philando Castile's murder, how he stood right next to Castile's window and didn't feel the need to pull his gun but then did nothing as his partner turned belligerent and fired round after round into Castile's car. Or the officer who watched as his partner dragged Anthony Promvongsa from his car, punched and kneed him, threw him to the ground, and continued to pummel him. There are countless videos of officers murdering, maiming, and beating BIPOC and shouting, "Stop resisting. Stop resisting." Notice how often their partners stand meekly by as they brutalize an unconscious BIPOC body unable to resist. Think of Dave Grossman, a police trainer who has become a kind of celebrity, who on camera "tells his students that the sex they have after they kill another human being will be the best sex of their lives," as Radley Balko notes in his review of the documentary *Do Not Resist* in the *Washington Post*. All these terrifying thoughts, these facts of American life, ran through my mind during a simple traffic stop.

I could go on, but you already know. We already know. Say their names. You know them by heart the same way I do. The only conclusion a sane person can reach is that the state wants us to always feel this terror. With each passing day, it feels like there are more people on the side of this madness than people who would see it end.

Black Lives Matter. Black Lives Matter. Black Lives Matter.

Men Don't Cry

On Toxic Masculinity

Years ago, I thought I was suffering from depression. I had financial and career troubles, and I was running six miles a day to cope. I spent most of my time feeling a deep sense of anger and despair, and I was unable to purge it. I tried to write it out, threw myself into writing poetry. *"Poet, heal thyself"* and all of that. I participated in three separate "thirty poems in thirty days" groups and wrote a series of poems that would become my first book. Eventually, I realized I was dealing with a crippling, deadly disease that must be taken seriously: toxic masculinity. I believed that I wasn't a man's man, that I wasn't a good provider for my family, that I wasn't a successful writer. I was allowing expectations—those of others and my own—to poison me.

*

There I was, a barely employed adjunct professor. I'd written a bunch of poems my friends were raving about. I sensed that the poems themselves were on the verge of crying but couldn't. I solicited feedback from a fellow poet, and she noted that the poems were detached, even disaffected. They were full of *void*. She said to me, "Have you read Lorde's 'Uses of the Erotic'? Do, immediately, okay? That right and wise argument that the erotic force is the creation force is the creative force is the volcano of god. Volcano—burning fires."

I read Audre Lorde's essay immediately. I'm not ashamed to say I was moved close to tears. The erotic, what Lorde calls "the personification of love in all its aspects—born of chaos, and personifying creative power and harmony," lay entombed and mummified in me, and that part of myself, that "I," was missing from my writing.

Let us take a step back before we go any further. Let us remember that men usurp every good thing. "Uses of the Erotic" was written to empower, educate, inform, and motivate women, especially women of color. Lorde writes, "When I speak of the erotic, then, I speak of it as an assertion of the lifeforce of women; of that creative energy empowered, the knowledge and use of which we are now reclaiming in our language, our history, our dancing, our loving, our work, our lives."

I have read Lorde's essay, studied it, and gained from it a new understanding of my life as a writer, and as a man. I must give credit where credit is due. *I thank you, Ms. Lorde, truly. I ask to partake of your table.*

* *

Feeling is essential to every part of my being. But, as a poet, I've struggled to accept that to feel is everything. I still have so much to learn.

Tears are a physical response, one born from emotion. The journey to deconstruct the obstruction—the one that prevents tears, sympathy, empathy, and feelings of vulnerability—is humanity's great struggle, and this is especially true for men. We are conditioned to feel less. We are told throughout our lives that we must not let our emotions control us, not allow sentimentality to influence how we choose our circle of friends or our careers or even our choice of partner. Men are expected to be stoic, hard, and cold. The trash patriarchal world we live in rarely rewards men who reveal their vulnerabilities, or their traumas.

When I decided to get serious about writing poetry, I applied to and then enrolled in an MFA program. It was in my MFA program that I began to realize how solid and impervious my emotional walls were. There is an "I" and an eye in great poetry. Accepting that binary,

exploring it to its profoundest depths, requires the erotic. I was completely disconnected from the erotic.

In her essay "Poetry Is Not a Luxury," Lorde writes, "I speak here
of poetry as a revelatory distillation of experience, not the sterile word
play that, too often, the white fathers distorted the word *poetry* to
mean—in order to cover a desperate wish for imagination without
insight." As a novice poet, I was failing to achieve the depth and
feeling required for my work to grow. I was avoiding the necessary
sacrifice of bleeding my blood through the ink. I didn't know where
the erotic was in my life, much less within me. I'd foolishly believed
that the erotic was strictly an external, sexual sensation. The realization that I'd been incorrect was terrifying because I didn't know
where to begin my journey into the true erotic.

But that was it, the *realization*. Lorde writes, "The erotic is a measure between the beginnings of our sense of self, and the chaos of our
strongest feelings." With the realization that I was closed off, I recognized my fear of what I might find if I knocked down my walls was
dooming my journey into the erotic. After that I had to allow myself
to be vulnerable, but being vulnerable, exposing yourself in any meaningful way, is a herculean challenge. Lorde writes, "It is never easy to
demand the most from ourselves, from our lives, from our work."

I went on the dark journey into the self and learned more than
could reasonably fit in one essay. However, the most difficult thing
I did not learn was how to cry. My inability to cry remained at the
heart of my being disconnected from the erotic. Crying is still a physically painful experience for me; afterward, my head and chest hurt,
there is a thumping at the back of my throat, and I'm disoriented and
exhausted. I continue to suppress tears whenever possible. Somewhere
in the farthest reaches of my soul I equate crying with failure, shame,
and weakness to such an extent that my body punishes me for it.
Think about that. Don't feel sorry for me, but if you're a man reading
this essay, or the mother or father of a son, ask yourself how deadly
this shame can make navigating stressful conditions. It is especially
toxic if you're also suffering from trauma. If you're an Afro-Latinx or
African American man, you need to know that it is also killing us.

* * *

Picture the white men raised with this idea of manhood holding leadership positions and dealing with America's complex landscape of race, economic status, religion, sexual orientation, and political affiliation. Go no further than the forty-fifth president of the United States of America—a man incapable of coherency, a man whose very speech pattern is reminiscent of a troubled and angry adolescent desperate for approval. He is the leader of a political system rotting internally from toxic masculinity.

For any man who aims to study, navigate, understand, and respect the differences in his world, being walled off and emotionless leads to frustration, humiliation, and confusion. It leads to hurting people. In the absence of expressive emotion, a psychotic anger will fester. Unfortunately, when a man doesn't understand, empathize, or sympathize with the multifarious nature of our world, he takes his place against the true erotic. He produces a reactionary toxic masculinity. One can argue that, on some level, mass shooters, many of whom struggle with various untreated mental health issues, also suffer from toxic masculinity. And by extension, one might argue that this is true of terrorists of all nations and faiths—ISIS, the Ku Klux Klan, Neo-Nazis, the Westboro Baptist Church and its adherents—as well as rapists, sexual abusers, and men living with suicidal ideation. They are all suffering from toxic masculinity.

Again, let us go back. According to Lorde, "The erotic is a resource within each of us that lies in a deeply female and spiritual plane, firmly rooted in the power of our unexpressed or unrecognized feeling." Too many men are indoctrinated into the school of suppression, repression, and aggression from an early age.

Some people argue that men have organic predispositions to anger and aggression; one thing that cannot be denied is that these emotions are unnaturally magnified and overdeveloped by a capitalist society that perpetuates toxic masculinity. Lorde writes:

> The principal horror of any system which defines the good in terms of profit rather than in terms of human need, or which defines human need to the exclusion of the psychic and emotional components of that need—the principal horror of such a system is that it robs our work of its erotic value, its erotic power and life appeal and fulfillment.

The most popular video games in America are first-person shooter games. Almost 30 percent of gamers are under the age of eighteen. On average, players kill "enemy" after "enemy" for at least three hours a day. The lines between reality and the virtual world become blurred. Young men learn to *expect* sex from women, and on some level, to crave and anticipate violence. And video games are only one example. We must also consider influences like film, television, commercial media, music, pornography, the fashion industry, cultural and ethnic traditions, and religion. Men in this country are steeped in toxic masculinity from the get-go.

Again, consider that these men go on to occupy positions of authority; these negative traits they've developed become weaponized against women and children, as well as other men. Humanity's, and especially men's, inability to channel the erotic is, I believe, the principal reason we live in an unbalanced world.

* * * *

As I read Lorde's work, I kept coming back to my own self, reasoning out why I cried so easily as a child. In my spiritual plane the erotic was virginal, hypersensitive, and wanting nourishment and development. But the world around us seeks to pervert the erotic within us, and our parents, God bless them, want us to be survivors, so they facilitate this erosion. Recently, a face painter on social media shared an experience they had with a boy and his parents. A young boy came up to her and wanted a butterfly painted on his face. His mother said no. She then turned to her husband and asked, "Do you want your son to have a butterfly on his face?" The husband replied, "No." They ended up painting a skull and crossbones on his face.

Lorde writes, "As women, we have come to distrust that power which rises from our deepest and non-rational knowledge." It shouldn't come as a surprise that my mother tried to quell the erotic within me, having already silenced the erotic within herself. And so, the cycle continues. When I was a boy, my mother would always yell at me for crying. "Men don't cry! Toughen up!" I never had to pick up my plate when I was done eating, never washed a dish, never cleaned up after myself at all. My grandmother, may she rest in peace, would say to me, "As long as there's a woman in the house, you should never have to clean." While recovering from the effects of toxic masculinity, the matriarchs in my family simultaneously perpetuated it.

When he was younger, I would yell at my own son to stop crying, to toughen up. I would ask him, "Is someone beating you? No, so stop crying." I was using his pain, what he was experiencing, against him to stop him from crying, from feeling. That was a horrible thing to do. Now, I pull him close for a hug. I allow him to let the tears fall, and we work through it together. We must allow our children to feel, and to express their feelings honestly.

In a 2010 *Psychology Today* article, Dr. Judith Orloff writes:

> Our bodies produce three kinds of tears: reflex, continuous, and emotional. Each kind has different healing roles. For instance, reflex tears allow your eyes to clear out noxious particles when they're irritated by smoke or exhaust. The second kind, continuous tears, are produced regularly to keep our eyes lubricated . . . Typically, after crying, our breathing, and heart rate decrease, and we enter into a calmer biological and emotional state.
>
> Emotional tears have special health benefits. Biochemist and "tear expert" Dr. William Frey at the Ramsey Medical Center in Minneapolis discovered that . . . emotional tears also contain stress hormones which get excreted from the body through crying . . . emotional tears shed these hormones and other toxins which accumulate during stress.

The word "toxins" sounds a four-alarm fire. There's a reason it's called toxic masculinity. Toxic masculinity can be physically lethal—and not just for the men and boys suffering from it, but for the people around them as well.

We must facilitate the expression of the erotic, the integration of the feminine, in our young boys so that they grow up to be better men. So that they can be capable of vulnerable emotion. As Lorde writes: "Recognizing the power of the erotic within our lives can give us the energy to pursue genuine change within our world . . . For not only do we touch our most profoundly creative source, but we do that which is female and self-affirming in the face of a racist, patriarchal, and anti-erotic society."

Traveling Freely

Like most parents, when I'm asked to travel for business, I experience mixed feelings. On the one hand, it's exciting to visit new and interesting places. I enjoy meeting people and learning about their lives and where they live. On the other hand, in this instance I was going to miss my son's playoff basketball game. His team had one victory and ten losses; they were the eighth seed, and more than likely, they were going to get squashed. I felt I should be there to see it, to cheer him on in the face of defeat, to mourn the loss with him. This trip also coincided with Father's Day. Even though I'd be back in time for Sunday, I'd miss some activities. My youngest daughter's daycare was having a Father's Day appreciation BBQ. My oldest daughter would be peppering me with questions to determine the most useful gift to buy me.

However, tenure-track teaching positions are hard to come by. So, when I was asked to go to a professional development conference to bolster my faculty file, I bought my Amtrak ticket and set out for Baltimore, Maryland. At Penn Station in Newark, New Jersey, I entered the Hudson newsstand and searched for an interesting book to read on the train. I looked for a while and didn't find one. I wasn't discouraged, because once upon a time, at Miami International Airport, I'd found Junot Díaz's *The Brief Wondrous Life of Oscar Wao* after digging for an hour. I went deep into the back of the store. The cashier craned her neck to see what I was doing. On the racks were various magazines featuring articles on ISIS, Iran, Syria, Greece, and the terrorist attacks on France and Belgium. Their titles questioned America's foreign policy and our ability to deal with difficult situations abroad.

I felt the familiar outrage that courses through me whenever I come across this subject. Journalists' refusal to look at America's domestic policy in the same light as its foreign policy drives me mad. American politicians have made a mess of poverty-stricken urban and rural America.

I overpaid for a Moleskine notebook and stepped outside to watch the departure screen. As a hyphenated American traveling (somewhat) freely around the East Coast, I think I know a lot about American foreign policy. It is eerily like American domestic policy in how it:

- Removes money and resources from people the state doesn't like
- Kills the people the state doesn't like
- Gives the money and resources to people the state does like
- Sprinkles in some violence intermittently to terrorize the people it took money and resources from
- Blames the people it took from for their situation
- Gives the story to the media to spin, twist, and exploit in perpetuity

I've seen this formula repeated countless times in the last year: in Ferguson, Missouri, for instance, or pick a city in Florida, Texas, California, New York, and on and on. My social media feeds are full of videos of police shootings (state-sanctioned murders) and judicial corruption. My email account is clogged with Change.org petitions asking for help reversing unjustified convictions and outrageous prison sentences. And it was not lost on me that I was going to Baltimore, where Freddie Gray sustained fatal injuries to his spine while riding handcuffed in a police van. There were protests, and some escalated into riots. I was happy about the way protesters and public officials decried the media coverage. Protesters shouted down Fox News reporter Geraldo Rivera, and Baltimore City Council President Jack Young lambasted media coverage as largely negative and as depicting African Americans according to negative stereotypes. Social media gorged on links, rants, shares, and arguments.

I grew up in neighborhoods like East and West Baltimore. When residents of those communities protested to voice their anger and frustration at being disenfranchised for so long, I didn't find it thuggish or criminal. I've always wondered what's taken our communities so long to react. Violence is a large and terrible part of surviving America's ghettos. There are precious few chances to better ourselves. I am honestly baffled that the violence doesn't spill out into open rebellion on picturesque Main Streets. Folks in Baltimore know this reality all too well. As Ta-Nehisi Coates writes in his award-winning book *Between the World and Me*:

> To be black in the Baltimore of my youth was to be naked before the elements of the world, before all the guns, fists, knives, crack, rape, and disease. The nakedness is not an error, nor pathology. The nakedness is the correct and intended result of policy, the predictable upshot of people forced for centuries to live under fear.

America's domestic policy is even more imperialistic than its policy abroad (not that it's a contest; both are tyrannical and wrong). There are few opportunities for *free* travel between classes, races, or American poverty. In his article in the *New Yorker*, "The Mobility Myth," James Surowiecki writes, "Seventy per cent of people born into the bottom quintile of income distribution never make it into the middle class, and fewer than ten per cent get into the top quintile. Forty per cent are still poor as adults."

I took a deep breath and tried to remember that this business trip would include some pleasure. I'd be meeting my dear friend Sean Morrissey, a poet and social justice worker in Baltimore, an activist with emphasis on the active, and a fellow skateboarder. It would be good to catch up, have a few drinks, talk poetry and, inevitably, politics. As interested as I was in learning everything I could about accelerated developmental education at the collegiate level, understanding what was happening in Baltimore became equally interesting.

These thoughts banged around in my head as I leafed through my new, blank, and overpriced Moleskine notebook. I started to write.

*

Penn Station in Baltimore is remarkably like Penn Station in Newark, but smaller. People go back and forth after trains, cabs, or buses.

Capitalism's castoffs sleep in corners on the floor and ask travelers if they can spare any change. The ones our society has truly ignored, the indigent and mentally ill, stare off into space and have conversations with no one. I catch a cab to the hotel. Along the way I recognize a similar city and similar signs: NOW LEASING, LOFTS FOR RENT, FULLY RENOVATED, NEW UNITS AVAILABLE—CALL TODAY. I recognize familiar faces of people trying to hold on—security guards, cashiers, sandwich makers. They wait for the bus or the light-rail, or they walk slowly on the shaded side of the street. And then there are the faces of people who have more than they need. I have been both the person holding on and the person with more than he needs, and as a native New Yorker I can spot gentrification with a blindfold on. Yet another American domestic policy, the goal of gentrification is to revitalize working-class or impoverished neighborhoods by pushing their residents out and introducing wealthy and mostly white new residents.

I risk the cliché and strike up a conversation with the cab driver, Raja. I confirm the area is indeed being gentrified, and he adds that he lived and drove cabs in New York City for many years. "The first American city I experienced when I arrived at US in 1983," Raja said. I expressed my disgust at gentrification, but he recalled a crime-riddled Harlem and a 42nd Street where drugs were sold and sex work was practiced out in the open, under the vigilance of abusive pimps. He even remembered that a cop once encouraged him to buy some marijuana, to loosen up. Raja argued that gentrification is great for lowering crime. I lamented the loss of African American and Latinx businesses. Shouldn't those business owners be rewarded for enduring in the face of crime and economic hardship? Didn't they give back to their communities by maybe floating some credit here and there? What a shitty reward after so many years, to be booted out of your lease to make space for another Starbucks or a Whole Foods. We carried on about the economic sustainability of gentrification and of soaring rents, wondering how long even the parents of white millennial gentrifiers could afford to pay New York prices.

We made our way down Charles Street. The Mount Vernon section of Baltimore reminded me a lot of Jersey City, Hoboken, University Heights in Newark, and of course, Harlem and Brooklyn. "What really alarms me," Raja said, "is the amount of young people begging for money in the street." I had seen them too: men and women between the ages of eighteen and forty, many of them white, with paper cups in their hands, asking for change. Some were struggling with addiction, while others ran the gamut: unemployed, mentally ill, unhoused. Raja explained that some street corners were full of young panhandlers and that they'd often rotate in shifts. He became nostalgic and said that America must create more jobs for people. I pointed out that if any of these young people had criminal records, finding a job would be next to impossible. "We have to do better," he said quietly. We arrived at the hotel, and I paid the fare with the corporate card the purchasing department gave me for this trip. My privilege and the fact that I was there for an education conference were not lost on me. Raja encouraged me to enjoy the Inner Harbor, stroll the boardwalk, and more importantly, "have some crab cakes." I thought of Nina Simone's mournful but funky rendition of "Baltimore," which describes the city as a "hard town by the sea," where nothing is for free.

* *

I met with Sean around 8:00 p.m. As we drove to dinner, I looked up at the skyscrapers already in place and the ones under construction. The Domino Sugar refinery, an anachronism surrounded by monoliths that made it look even more out of place, surprised me. Domino had managed to maintain sugar production in the face of growing competition and, more importantly, had managed to sustain blue-collar jobs. America desperately needs more good-paying blue-collar jobs. Sean explained that aside from corporations like Legg Mason and Lupin, Baltimore was home to Kevin Plank, the founder and CEO of Under Armour. Plank's development signs were all over Baltimore: SAGAMORE DEVELOPMENT. They appeared in the Inner Harbor and around the site of another, much larger, "multiuse facility" planned in the Port Covington section of Baltimore.

The Port Covington project had warning signs all over it. Sagamore Development was asking Baltimore for millions to get the project done. It would receive this money in the form of a TIF. The *Journal of Property Tax Assessment & Administration* defines a TIF this way:

Through the use of TIFs municipalities typically divert future property tax revenue increases from a defined area or district toward an economic development project or public improvement project in the community. The first TIF was used in California in 1952. By 2004 all 50 American States had authorized the use of TIF.

According to Natalie Sherman's *Baltimore Sun* article "BDC Moves Forward 535 Million Port Covington TIF," the Baltimore Development Corporation was all too eager to push the project through.

> Keisha Allen, president of the Westport Neighborhood Association, said she understands why Sagamore has asked for city financing, but she wants to see further scrutiny of the request. "It just seems like it was already a done deal," she said. "I don't want them to just push it through. I want them to do a little homework and make sure that we're OK with it." The BDC board, which is composed of city officials and professionals from firms such as T. Rowe Price Group and M&T Bank, gave a green light to the TIF request after three committee meetings, much of which was closed to the public, and less than an hour of discussion on Thursday.

Surrounding communities are justified in their concerns. Sagamore Development is asking for a lot of money. What is most problematic is where projects that receive TIFs choose to develop. None of the developers that received TIF benefits have revitalized traditionally African American communities in East or West Baltimore. All the projects take place in and around the Inner Harbor. According to Baltimore Rising.org, "Where they [TIF projects] aren't is in the city's disadvantaged neighborhoods that are desperate for employment and commerce." To complicate matters, the BDC operates largely in the shadows. Again, from Baltimore Rising.org:

> The BDC . . . is an independent, non-profit 501(c)(3) organization under contract with the city. It is noticeably reluctant to release information about how it picks the projects it funds and the success of those projects financially, for the

neighborhoods in which they are located and for the city overall.

There were more than 535 million tax dollars on the line, a fact not lost on former state planning director Ron Kreitner. "The magnitude of this so far exceeds anything even considered, it just begs for going the extra mile in terms of protecting the taxpayers," he's quoted as saying in Sherman's piece. "This is so far removed from transparent government operations that it's very disturbing."

After dinner, Sean and I walked the streets of Mount Vernon. The enclaves in a city never surprise me: Latinxs on one block, African Americans on another, Asians on another, and so on. Perhaps because I never saw white people wanting to live where I lived, it still jars me to see hipsters, yoga mat carriers, and running-shorts-wearing twentysomethings among the enclaves. They pop up out of nowhere with long beards and extra-small polo shirts. But gentrification in Baltimore works a little differently than it does in the cities I know. A notable percentage of the people displaced by gentrification here are working-poor and lower-middle-class whites. The gentrifiers are middle- to upper-middle-class college-educated workers, and among them are representative minorities. However, the dissonance between these groups is all too similar.

On the streets, there is no acknowledgement between the different groups. There is a lot of walking head down by whites to avoid making eye contact with perceived minorities. I suppose you could attribute this to avoiding panhandlers (white or otherwise), but I've seen the same avoidance on NYC streets. I question when it became chic to live in a city—to claim that city as your own but to live within it in a completely disengaged way. These days it's popular to say, "I live in Brooklyn" (or Flatbush, or Bed-Stuy, or Harlem, or Baltimore, and so on). Millennials, hipsters, and artists equate living in these cities with edginess and grit. They want the prestige of living in culturally rich, economically challenged, and diverse communities, but without engaging within them. Instead, gentrifiers blame minority residents for the economic disparities and blight of their communities.

Disturbingly, more and more white millennials are racist. The *Washington Post* reports, "When it comes to explicit prejudice against blacks, non-Hispanic white millennials are not much different than whites belonging to Generation X (born 1965–1980) or Baby Boomers (born 1946–1964)." This is the generation of whites that was supposed to start dismantling white supremacy. However, too many millennials seem content to keep benefiting from it. Sean told me about the ways white millennials stereotype minorities and the racial remarks he's heard: "They're so ghetto, they can't speak English, and they're lazy." He may be white, but Sean is a solid ally. In an era where progressive racism is a plague in the white community, you can't take shit like that for granted. We laughed at the way white millennials who grew up watching television shows like *In Living Color* and *Chappelle's Show* missed the point. Those comedians were satirizing the way white people caricaturized minorities; they weren't providing whites with a cultural education. In part, they were saying, "Look how you fools view us." For too many, the depictions of minorities they saw then and continue to see now have become dogma. Likewise, too many white millennials have failed to contextualize the civil rights movement, institutionalized racism, and white privilege.

Sean and I end the night over a few bourbons. We know we can't solve all the world's problems, but we can make sure we know what they are. Our ignorance is not a source of bliss.

* * *

The next day I attend presentations, breakout sessions, and workshops. A piece of data from one of the presentations was relevant to my ruminations. At least 80 percent of students in community college remedial courses are African American or Latinx. Over 50 percent of full-time faculty at community colleges are white women, and although I couldn't find exactly how many of them teach developmental education, I'm sure the number is higher than 50 percent. Many of them are what the industry calls "graying" faculty, aged sixty or older. An *Inside Higher Ed* article reveals "the divisions where faculty members were staying around well past 70 featured professors in the humanities, arts, natural and physical sciences and education, among others." The national push is for accelerated and integrated developmental courses. Instead of making students take three or four remedial classes before they can enroll in credit-earning courses, students would take one remedial course and then an integrated remedial and credit-earning course. The federal government wants students to get more bang for their student loan buck, and I don't blame them.

I am troubled by the *Washington Post*'s data on millennials and race. I wonder what percentage of teachers in developmental courses, be they millennials, Gen Xers, or baby boomers, share similar racist ideas about minorities—in particular, racist ideas about laziness and lack of intelligence. Unfortunately, academic hiring of minorities is suspect to begin with. According to Colleen Flaherty's *Inside Higher Ed* article "Demanding 10 Percent," the numbers aren't encouraging: "A wider analysis by the Associated Press found that no state's flagship public university campus had a black faculty population approaching 10 percent, and that only a few topped 5 percent. Most campuses were between 2 and 4 percent."

As more full-time tenure-track positions disappear every day, remedial students may not see more minority teachers in the classroom anytime soon. At lunch, as I stood on the buffet line, I overheard a presenter (who was white) telling an Asian professor that her new homeopathic doctor, "a Chinese lady," had severely restricted her diet. She said all of this in a caricaturized Asian accent. I continue to worry about our progress in the field of education. How many times has she done something insensitive like this in class?

After a full day at the conference, I was back on Baltimore's streets with Sean. We talked about his work with the Right to Housing Alliance. Sean and a host of volunteers worked in conjunction with the Public Justice Center to write *Justice Diverted: How Renters Are Processed in the Baltimore City Rent Court.* The report was made available to the public via the internet.

> Our study shows that the court system prioritizes efficiencies which privilege the landlord's bottom line, and as a result, it decidedly ignores two predominating realities of poor renters and their housing. First, renters lack access to timely legal advice and have insufficient knowledge to navigate the process.
>
> Second, renters are poor, have few rental options other than Baltimore's crumbling housing stock, and look to the court to enforce housing standards. Our data show that Rent Court defendants are among the most vulnerable people in

the city. Most are Black women, living on $2,000 or less per month, without public housing assistance.

Evictions exacerbate houselessness. Houselessness is another critical issue facing Baltimore and major cities across America. I wonder if judges, lawyers, property owners, or developers read this report. I wonder how deep their apathy goes. In neighborhoods across both East and West Baltimore, vacant buildings line city block after city block. Surely, Kevin Plank and Sagamore Development, just to name one, could propose safe and affordable housing to the residents of these communities. Shouldn't TIF benefits be prioritized for the communities in most need? Gentrification, for good or bad, has completely missed neighborhoods like Ellwood Park, Baltimore Highlands, Patterson Park, Monument Street, Orangeville, and Madison-Eastend. The residents of these communities deserve the same opportunities as those in the Inner Harbor. Have you given up on them, Baltimore?

It's mind-boggling that a city with such fiscal demands and needs would approve an almost six-hundred-million-dollar TIF for a development project. Baltimore Mayor Stephanie Rawlings-Blake struggled to balance the budget without cutting critical education programs. Think of how six hundred million dollars from development projects could have saved the budget. Sean keenly observed that city and state governments concede too much to corporate interests. They act powerless in the face of the corporate money machine and offer sweetheart deals, one after another, at the taxpayer's expense. This same scenario plays out across America. In a 2012 *New York Times* article, Louise Story writes:

> A *Times* investigation has examined and tallied thousands of local incentives granted nationwide and has found that states, counties and cities are giving up more than $80 billion each year to companies. The beneficiaries come from virtually every corner of the corporate world, encompassing oil and coal conglomerates, technology and entertainment companies, banks and big-box retail chains.

I thought again of foreign and domestic policy, and of all the social justice workers like Sean fighting to make change. They're doing research and drafting reports that prove inequity and injustice; they're writing essays and doing community service. They're trying to stem the tide of corruption, greed, apathy, and violence that's consuming our country. The most frustrating aspect of the work they do has to be that their services are readily available, yet few people seek them out. Healthcare for the Homeless, Our Daily Bread, Right to Housing Alliance, and countless other organizations are working for the people of Baltimore. We must look, and help.

* * * *

My last day in Baltimore Sean dropped me off at Penn Station, and I gave him a long hug. I let him know how moved I was at his almost complete disavowal of consumerism and his dedication to serve others. I boarded the train and looked forward to seeing my family. When I'd get home, I'd hug them and kiss my wife. Then my kids would ask me about my trip. They'd want to know what I saw and what I did. My oldest would ask me if I heard about the gay nightclub massacre in Orlando. And as I would search for words to answer their questions, I'd also be thinking about how America, with all our talk of democracy and liberty, is an extremist country. I'd have to explain that the middle ground, the middle class, bipartisan agreement, commonsense legislation, and socioeconomic policies are being squeezed out of existence. In America, it isn't enough that we all have the right to own a gun; the right to own a gun must supersede common sense, logic, and fail-safes. It isn't enough to make a double or triple profit; American corporations want ten times the normal profit. Injustice travels freely across America, more freely even than her citizens. And our cities are the same as the countries where America practices its foreign policy. Our cities are laboratories where genocidal economic and political policies become sport for the powerful.

The police officers responsible for the injuries that killed Freddie Gray have been acquitted of all charges. Baltimore State's Attorney Marilyn Mosby held an impassioned press conference where she condemned members of the Baltimore police force for obstructing her office's investigation. A colleague of mine is a lawyer, and he questioned why Mosby would charge the officers with homicide as opposed to criminal negligence. However, Mosby has pursued questionable convictions and supported the Baltimore police's lethal arrest methods before. Recently, Mosby's office pushed to convict Keith Davis, a Baltimore man shot in the face by police for allegedly possessing a gun. Eyewitness and police testimony were conflicting and nonsensical. Mosby's office still charged Davis with fifteen separate charges.

Mosby's press conference in response to the acquittal of the officers in Freddie Gray's death drew enthusiastic support. However, we must look at her entire body of work before proclaiming her a hero. By the same token, the police officers sworn to protect and serve us cannot continue to be called unequivocal heroes until they start policing their own. I'm reminded of D. Watkins's *The Beast Side*:

> The police officers in Baltimore, as in many places in the country with dense black populations, are out of control and have been out of control. One of the major reasons is that many Baltimore police officers don't live in Baltimore City; some don't even live in Maryland. Many don't know or care about the citizens of the communities they police, which is why they can come in, beat us, and kill us without a sign of grief or empathy.

If there were empathy or even mercy, perhaps Freddie Gray would be alive, and the countless others who have died at the hands of the police would still be here. Perhaps.

Distraction

Bob Hicok's Essay as Poetry's MAGA Moment

The very serious function of racism . . . is distraction. It keeps you from doing your work.

—Toni Morrison, "A Humanist View," at Portland State University

This response will be quick, for I will not allow racism to keep me from my work. However, I will call racism out. My people—the ones I call friends in real life and the ones I fuck with on social media—don't need to have racism explained to them. Neither do I. We know. Nor do we need to justify our abundance, our talents, our stories, our blessups, or our work. We know. This response is about not allowing people to get away with shit. Periodt.

Hicok's essay, "The Promise of American Poetry," published in *Utne*, is a restatement of "Make America Great Again," but this time for heterosexual male poets who believe they are white. I'm supposed to say, "whether he intended to or not," but I won't. I'm tired of presuming that the white people who write racist essays might simultaneously be innocent. Not today, Bob. Hicok believes he's "dying as a poet" because he doesn't sell the same number of books he's used to or see his books reviewed as often. He goes on to imply that because cis hetero white males have been notorious gatekeepers, they're getting their comeuppance and being relegated to the sidelines. "Inevitable," he writes, as he bemoans the changing color of poetry and poets. Hicok writes that as a child of the sixties he's all for progress (yes, he mentions the Kennedys, Kent State, and Dr. King's "I Have a Dream" speech) but wonders how he should feel about not being part of the dominant group anymore.

As I reread Hicok's essay, I can't help but hear a more polished and articulate Trump. Hicok is telling this generation of male heterosexual poets who believe they are white to be wary, that minorities are replacing them. And not just on the page, at poetry readings, and on bookshelves, but in America as well, as a demographic. Yeah, he tries to use his white liberal ideology as a counterweight to his racism, but no. It doesn't work. It's old hat.

I also hear lurking within the passive-aggressive lines of Hicok's essay the voices of the Charlottesville racists: "You will not replace us." It echoes Fox News's rhetoric about the shrinking white majority (cue horror movie scream). In their *New York Times* article, "White 'Power' and the Fear of Replacement," Abigail Levin and Lisa Guenther explain what "you will not replace us" means. They argue that the phrase becomes "another way of reasserting the supremacy of whiteness and its irreplaceable, but precarious, value in a fundamentally confused zero-sum game where one group's gain must equal another group's loss." Hicok is stating that he is dying as a poet because we— Black, Latinx, POC, LGBTQ+, Muslim, Indigenous, and othered writers—are flourishing. I recall a quote attributed to Richard Nixon and Southern Strategy politics: "You have to face the fact that the whole problem is really the blacks. The key is to devise a system that recognized this while not appearing to."

Hicok's dog whistles could embolden gatekeepers to reduce the already small percentages of *us* that they welcome through their doors. Despite his sobs for the diminished and dying white poet, publishing overall is 79 percent white, and that depends on whom you ask. Some organizations record a higher number. In 2015, Jennifer Baker reported in *Forbes*, "Lee & Low Books released the results of the first Diversity Baseline Survey confirming the lack of representatives from marginalized cultures throughout the industry as well as within various levels including executive, editorial, sales, marketing and publicity, and book reviews." Here's one of their graphics showing the lack of representation in the industry overall:

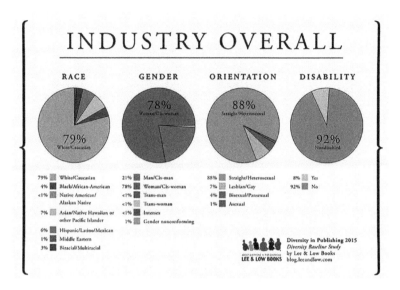

And here is a graphic showing the breakdowns of those reviewers Bob is lusting after:

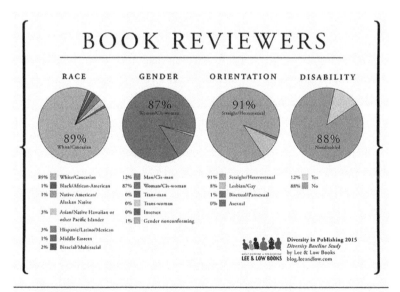

Diversity Baseline Survey (DBS) 2015

Survey planning by Jason Low, Lee & Low Books, Publisher/Co-owner; Hannah Ehrlich, Lee & Low Books, Director of Marketing & Publicity

Reporting and Data measurement by Sarah Park Dahlen, St. Catherine University MLIS Program Assistant Professor; Nicole Catlin, St. Catherine University MLIS Program Graduate Assistant

Special Thanks to Jeremy M. Friedman, Evaluation Consultant; James Smith, Counsel, Litigation for Labor & Employment, Kilpatrick Townsend & Stockton LLP; Gregory Wong, legal counsel; Kevin Wong, legal counsel

*

Whiteness centers itself as the victim in issues where whiteness is the perpetrator of harm. This self-centering is whiteness's chief super-power; it is hellbent on establishing its innocence. Perhaps this is why Hicok keeps lathering on the sappy "I'm a liberal" rhetoric between his recurring racism. He's trying to prove his innocence, but by the end, it's an incoherent ramble. I can almost hear Dean Armitage glee-fully dropping "my man" before every small dose of racism. Or one of my favorites, "I would have voted for Obama a third time. Best presi-dent ever. Hands down," when he brings Dr. Martin Luther King Jr. into the essay. This essay could be a character in a Jordan Peele horror movie.

People who believe they are white cannot resist this power. White-ness is narcissistic, it is morbid, and it is addictive. In short, it's a helluva drug. Hicok does what white people often do: he reduces people of color and othered people to stereotypes about their identi-ties. He then credits their stereotyped identities for any success they might have achieved. But there is something else. Hicok is trying and failing to create a conflicted white identity. He is trying to mirror the very writing he claims is killing him as a poet, to duplicate our multi-faceted complexity. But Hicok cannot read our work outside of his privileged, racial power dynamic. Instead of being compelling, what he's published is proof of his desire to be the victim at our expense. In his article "Authenticity Obsession, or Conceptualism as Minstrel Show," Ken Chen writes, "It is not enough for the colonizer to own the world—the only thing missing, the only thing escaping his grasp, is to own the trauma that he himself authored."

Hicok has a lot of nerve to cry scarcity with a résumé that is so long and so lucrative. His tenth collection of poetry is out and about. Maybe he's charging his base. Hicok is urging the twenty-one- to forty-year-old heterosexual males who believe they are white to, hey, buy white, review white, and publish white. Oh, you so edgy, Bob, and racist, and not innocent at all. You know what you did with your essay. Poet Jenny Zhang writes, "The long con of white mediocrity may never be exposed . . ." At least, it may not be exposed by other white people. My folks and I have a saying: "If that person had a friend, then *dot dot dot*." If Hicok had a friend, they wouldn't have allowed him to publish that essay. However, it is more likely that he does have friends, and they agree with him.

Okay, I'm going back to work now.

Home

An Irrevocable Condition

I remember the streets. I remember the cracked and crooked sidewalks forming patterns like neurons. I've seen life through these patterns, made new forms, retreaded old ones, and used them all the time like stencils. Concrete is my sounding board, my adviser, and hardship my silent navigator. *No matter where you go, there you are.*

*

I live in the suburbs now. "The place," my friend says, "where married people go to die."

Yet I remember the two-family homes in my hood, leaning like they partied too hard—paint-chipped front doors with rat-chewed corners, rusted hinges on rotting wood, and big shiny new locks like the gold Jesus pieces on the Hustlers parked out front. The housing projects were a never-ending parade of bricks—warm and cozy in the winter, warm and cozy in the summer, and every season in between. Our faces began to resemble the bricks.

I remember the rooming house I shared with two addicts and how they'd roller-skate uphill all day long. There were also two sisters who looked nothing alike, one of whom had a baby, and when we got rowdy, they'd become silent and invisible. They shared the attic apartment with a haughty Argentine the addicts were coaching up from cocaine to crack. And I remember the pervert on the first floor with his underage-looking "friends." And the landlord with three daughters and two sons—the oldest barely nine years old—and his wife back in the motherland crying and sweating it out on Deportation Avenue. A nine-year-old will knock on the doors of strange and addled men to demand the rent. Rivers of malt liquor, blood, rum, and tears cut right through that house.

* *

I live in the suburbs now. I practice a new kind of survival—of symmetrical lawns that must be green, greener than the next and the next after that. And perfect. "Listen, why don't you use my guy?" "Because everyone on this street uses him." I shrug. The patches of barren dirt and no grass are my answer to all of this. A giant clock ticks here all the time. We kneel and worship the clock. We rise from bed, eat, go to work, eat, come home, eat, do the kid things, sleep, and do the same thing again the next day. The clock is a demanding god. He wants it done the same way every day. Here the neighbors say, "Be smart. Vote for Romney," or "You can't trust those people. They're terrorists, all of them," and they sprinkle in between, "How's it going?" This isn't the violence I'm used to. I live in the suburbs now, *myself, split open, unable to speak, in exile from myself.*

One day the bricks came out my pocket. You see, sometimes neighbors write litanies and believe you want to hear them. And on my small patch of miserable lawn, the one asymmetrical thing in the middle of all these perfectly manicured squares surrounded by driveways and BMWs, shaded by oak, chestnut, gum, and pine trees, the pattern of the concrete emerged. "You know," he started, "you should repave that sidewalk." Then added, ". . . and that siding could be power washed." After that, "You think you got enough garbage cans in your yard?" And "Around here we usually only keep two." And "This ain't Elizabeth, you know." And "You should be careful with all that sun you're getting. You're starting to look like Obama." He reared back for another one, and I jumped in on the beat, the one in my head. *What you eat don't make me shit.*

* * *

I remember my grandmother's mop stick. To play stickball, I'd use my grandmother's mop stick. To play fight on Saturdays, after the kung fu double feature, I'd use my grandmother's mop stick. I used a steak knife to cut it in three pieces, and with a shoelace from my sneakers and some duct tape made a three-section staff. I was the man on the block like, *Huh, allow me to demonstrate the skill of Shaolin!* It was worth the ass-whooping my grandmother gave me.

I remember my first full-time job—six bucks an hour under the table. I stopped drinking Olde English 800 malt. I still bought my food from the chicken shack. Commercial streets consisted of Korean-owned stores that sold imitations of name brands, chicken shacks owned by Middle Easterners, the occasional pizzeria or Chinese restaurant, and small liquor stores. On payday I walked down the long streets and bought twenty-two-ounce German beers, then hit the chicken shack for a huge beef rib slathered in barbecue sauce, a double cheeseburger, and a deep-fried chicken breast. Then I'd move along the stained, garbage-riddled streets to my hole-in-the-wall, *the working man's jackpot.* And when the beer ran out, I ran to the bodega. I can still hear merengue, bachata, salsa, and love ballads played over the sound of the deli meat slicer.

Night was the hook. The half-dead streetlamps created more darkness. And from the pitch-black side streets, the sudden alleyways and idling cars, violence exploded. Yes, I was afraid, but also alive. I got snuck (see: punched in the face unexpectedly) a few times. I regrouped with my posse and came back (see: large group and "Now what, bish?"). The cops were always around, making sure we stayed real chill. Content with scraps off capitalism's table—that we only howled at night, and that we only ate each other.

But the day was just as capricious. I remember a drug deal gone bad, in broad daylight; my friend "R," the drug dealer, got stabbed, and our posse chased after the crack fiend. I remember my friend Felix, blocks away, with fate guiding him to our turmoil, rounding the corner—a corner we'd turned thousands of times, a corner occupied by drunks from morning to evening and Monday through Sunday, beautiful women in minidresses jumping quickly in and out of cars on Friday and Saturday nights, and young hustlers in loud cars blowing kisses and hooting with no concept of time. Felix rounded that corner—his eyes always on the lookout for us. He saw us and the hate in our eyes in the background, and the object of that hate, the crackhead, in the foreground. And there was no time, no way to measure the brevity of that breath. He tried to help us, to stop that man, but there was no time. And the crackhead shanked him and took him. This is the violence nobody was used to, but we learned to expect it. I never lived here. I survived here.

* * * *

I live in the suburbs now. This is a different kind of survival, a different violence—here it is a perversion of idyll. We take and we want, we want and we have. Here there are toy lightsabers, Sony PlayStations, Nintendo Wii Us, Blu-ray players, flat-screen televisions, iPads, iPhones, MacBook Pros, and home alarm systems. Here there are baseball gloves, bats, cleats, basketballs, and pristine courts that have rims with nets. Here there is lacrosse. Food spoils in refrigerators, and kids aren't hungry at dinnertime. They aren't hungry. The streets here tell me nothing. And residents say the same things: "They're quiet, good people. They mind their own business. Their house always looks so nice." You can look, but you won't *see* anyone. We're all pronouns without antecedents here. Every house is quiet, neat, and unassuming. My grandmother taught me to fear what I can't see.

I live in the suburbs now. I worked hard for this, strove for this, yes sirred, no ma'amed, and overtimed for this. And I forget home for this—from time to time. Home is nothing to write love songs about: there is no romance, only the memory of hunger, adrenaline, pain, the growl of the wolves, and the cries of the meek.

American Violence

The first day of school is precious. If you are a parent, you plan for it, buy school supplies and new clothes and sneakers, and maybe, if it's still warm and not raining, you walk to school holding your child's hand. Before the pandemic would alter all our lives, I stood on the playground waiting for my child's teacher to show up, and I saw a man wearing a peculiar T-shirt. In white letters, on this T-shirt, was the roman numeral three encircled by a sphere of thirteen white stars. I recognized this, but at that moment, I didn't remember where from. After the meet and greets, and after the farewells and good lucks, I sat in my car and did a quick Google search: "roman numeral three encircled by stars." Three percenters, an anti-government militia. According to the Anti-Defamation League, "the term 'Three Percenter' refers to the erroneous belief that only 3% of colonists fought against the British during the Revolutionary War—but achieved liberty for everybody." Sounds about right. An organization of armed white men believing a false history to empower themselves to terrorize others.

I fell into a militia internet rabbit hole: Proud Boys, boogaloo boys, SovCits, and Oath Keepers. Google led me to an informative *New York Times* article by Leah Sottile called "The Chaos Agents." I encourage you to read it. Sottile's article led me to YouTube, then to Facebook, then Instagram, where the world of militiamen is on full display, conducting training exercises in the desert, in forests, on mountains, or at gun courses. YouTube videos teach two-man "tactical" teammates how to "sweep" a building or a room. How to cover an enormous amount of terrain in conjunction with drone support. How to plan an ambush or a frontal assault. And then, former military personnel like Navy SEALs, Army Rangers, and other elite soldiers for hire provide training on close-quarters combat, handling rifles, and knife fighting. These "private military contractors" sometimes work independently or for PMCs (private military companies, see Blackwater USA). Together they work as part of the privatized military industry, an industry with its tentacles into almost every country in the world. There is an entire cottage industry thriving off the PMC and American militia movements. The sales numbers for gun belts, ammo belts, first aid kits, bulletproof vests, bulletproof book bags for the kids, survival kits, knives, military clothing, and violent gadgets increase every day.

I'm sitting in my car; outside the air is cool, and I'm thinking about these men. I want to know who they're preparing to fight. They are everyone and everywhere. Given America's historical treatment of her citizens—of Indigenous people, African Americans, Asians, Latinx, Jews, and Muslims—I don't find it crazy to think militia members are preparing for people who look like me. I didn't see a lot of Black and brown faces in those militia videos. I saw white men who could be grocers, accountants, schoolteachers, and cops (see Charlottesville). American law enforcement agencies all agree the greatest threat for domestic terror is white men, and yet they do next to nothing about it. They allow these men to keep arming themselves and to play war games with live ammunition. Meanwhile, members of these very same law enforcement agencies are also members of militias and racist organizations. It is an open secret in America that white supremacists have infiltrated law enforcement. Knowing the historical context (the police were originally slave catchers), no one should be surprised to learn that active police officers supplement training that is already hyper-militarized with PMCs. Police supporters argue officers need militarized training in a society that refuses to control the number of guns that flow through its citizenry. I beg to differ; I've seen the videos of the Capitol riot. The people we need to worry about, who are ready to overthrow our government, are white folks. And then, of course, there are the mass shooters, the "lone wolves" who worship from afar and emulate white militancy.

*

It is dreadful to be
so violently dispersed.
To dare hope for nothing,
and yet dare to hope.
To know that hoping
and not hoping
are both criminal endeavors,
and, yet, to play one's cards.

—James Baldwin,
"Death is easy (for Jefe)"

I used to believe that I abhorred violence. Time has taught me quite
the opposite. As an American, I carry violence within me. I consume
and disseminate violence, whether I like it or not. Film, television,
entertainment, music, advertising, politics, government, law enforcement, and the judiciary commit us to violence daily. They keep us
in violence. As a Black man, I carry the violence committed against
my ancestors, throughout the Americas, in my DNA. We all keep
violence in the same way, deep down in our fibers. Here in America,
violence is a psychological process akin to the social media feedback
loop. You're either the doomscroller or the influencer.

Perhaps you're watching the news, reading news articles online, or
listening to the radio. You come across a story about *another* school
shooting or mass shooting. You scream to yourself that someone
should be doing something about this, but you're also paralyzed. Or
you say to yourself that if someone there had had a gun, they could
have done something. You say to yourself, *If I had been there, if I'd
had a gun, I would have done something, shot the shooter in the shoul-
der or the leg, or I would have killed the shooter.* Does it become a
daydream, a fantasy? How often do you do this? Fantasize about killing the killers? Fantasize about killing the people creating a perceived
controversy, causing you stress, making you unhappy, uncomfortable?
How quickly is violence the path forward for you? Or does it work in
reverse—are you terrified that you could be next, that you could be
at the receiving end of the gun? That the people, the problems, the
situations that cause you discomfort or real pain are coming to kill

you? And then you sit down to watch *John Wick*, *The Avengers*, movies from the *Saw* franchise. Each new blockbuster becomes more violent to top the last one, and we are ready. Take my money. We are living, breathing powder kegs. Whether we explode or implode depends on whether American violence has made us wolves or sheep.

Fearmongering is violence. In America, we are kept in a state of perpetual fear by the threat of violence. The truth is we are a desperately frustrated citizenry and a desperately oppressed people. But we have no way of articulating any of that desperation and oppression because we can't stop regurgitating the violence heaped on us by our oppressors. Every time a president or politician utters the words "This is America" as if we're some beacon in the sky of rightness and goodness, it is a form of violence. Our unemployment is close to 30 percent. We have an insane unhoused crisis because we have a mental health treatment crisis. The overwhelming majority of our population is working poor. Our police force is empowered to kill on sight with little to no repercussions, and the ultrarich freely control our political apparatus. All of this is violence, and what is worse still is pretending that none of it is true. If we are fed violence for entertainment and consume it freely, how can we process actual violence? That our government let so many of us die of COVID-19 is violence, that they let us die due to the unemployment, houselessness, and loss of health benefits that resulted from COVID-19 is violence.

All I have are questions. Some are rhetorical, while others require genuine answers that no one gives. I live in the suburbs. Many of the white men gearing up to drag America into either a race war or a civil war live in neighborhoods like mine—benign-looking block after block of neatly arranged houses, lawns, and cars. Grown white men who were once little boys playing cops and robbers and cowboys and Indians: maybe they had the cow-spotted hats, the aluminum six-shooter, the plastic badge, and handcuffs. Today, they have militia T-shirts and car stickers of American flags in the shape of the Punisher skull, with a blue stripe running down its side. They defiantly support a police force that has in its ranks racists committed to killing American minorities. David Masciotra, in his *Salon* article, "The Punisher Skull: Unofficial Logo of the White American Death Cult," articulates this phenomenon:

It is difficult to quantify with precision, but a large percentage of Americans, mostly white men, do not have the interpretive skill to comprehend a comic book, and as a consequence, are knowingly or unknowingly celebrating the symbol of a character who, if actually existed, would be a serial killer living as a fugitive from the law . . .

Americans who wear the Punisher skull signify spiritual fidelity to the dark heart of murder beating underneath the red, white and blue façade of American identity. They quietly observe reports on police shootings, drone strikes, and soldiers suffering from PTSD . . . they ritualize a fetishization of pain, terror and execution.

They keep playing their very real war games like children who refuse to grow up, and they bring all of it with them to the first day of school, to the office, to the polls.

Save the Babies

I used to be a catechist in the Catholic Church, or to say it a different way, I was a Sunday school teacher. My classes consisted of teaching third and fourth graders about the Eucharist and the sacraments from outdated workbooks. The curriculum taught nothing about the Bible, but I persevered for two years. Mostly, I deviated from the curriculum and explained each Bible book to the students and provided context about their authorship. I enjoyed the natural curiosity and wonder the children exuded in class. Because I was an adult, they trusted me. The children saw their parents chatting with me and shaking my hand before and after class. Sometimes the parents would be late picking them up, so I'd wait with them, sometimes for half an hour or more. The parents completely trusted the church, that their kids would be safe in our care. My students were sweet kids, and I was a different person then, full of blind faith.

Then the child sex abuse scandal broke out, and I broke with the church. Countless parishioners argued with me about supporting the church and not abandoning my faith. Their argument for accepting the sex abuse scandal as "not that serious" and "probably exaggerated" was ridiculous. "We're Catholic," they said. "We can't abandon the church." Every paper worth a damn published first-person accounts of the abuse. I watched at least four documentaries on the global reach of the church's sexual abuse, the duration of the abuse, and the ongoing cover-up. Yet these parishioners dismissed the horrors, as if saying "We're Catholic" was a shield against being a human being capable of independent thought and feeling. I left the church and never regretted it for a second.

Perhaps no other country in the West produces the kind of people America produces. Ta-Nehisi Coates calls them Dreamers in *Between the World and Me*: people completely disconnected from reality. Americans desperately cling to institutions for a sense of identity: religious, political, educational, economic, or socially constructed and nebulous. Americans, especially many European Americans (people who believe they are white), desperately want the power of certainty: to know for sure who they are, who "those" people over there are, what "they" do over there, and how and why what "we" do here is better. That's a catastrophic situation when you consider that American institutions speak of themselves as not only exceptional, but completely moral and righteous. They can do no wrong, nor have they ever wronged anyone. American institutions disavow the bloody reality that is American history and how that history of war and enslavement made them wealthy and powerful. (This is a chief reason why the Republican party is working so hard to discredit Nikole Hannah-Jones's *The 1619 Project* and ban critical race theory from the education system.) So it is that when Americans identify with institutions, we absolve ourselves of all responsibility. We are free not to care because we believe that we—like the institutions we are slaves to—are righteous and innocent. It is hard to wake up from this Dream, almost impossible.

When you know real American history, you're not surprised when the American government imprisons asylum seekers from South and Central American countries or targets immigrants from the Caribbean, East Asian countries, and African nations for deportation. When you know real American history, you are not surprised when children are separated from their parents and when both are put into cages, nor are you surprised to learn that prison corporations and weapons manufacturers are profiting from all of it. The American government, for over a hundred years, separated thousands of Native American children from their parents and communities and sent them to assimilation camps (benevolently known as boarding schools). The children were forcibly stripped of their language and identity and were punished for being demonstrably Indigenous. Horror stories of rape, physical abuse, and the terror of being removed from their families have all been documented. Americans' excuse at the time? Come now. Can't you hear them already? "We're civilized white people," or "This is a Christian nation," or perhaps the most telling, "We have to resolve the Indian problem." A uniquely American habit: create the problem of dislocated Indigenous people by stealing their land, and then terrorize them as part of the solution.

More Americans should read, so as not to be in a constant state of shock.

During slavery, children were stolen from their enslaved parents and sold off as a standard business practice. Countless generations scattered across the country to traumatize and destroy Black people's sense of humanity. America still hasn't come to grips with its racist past or present. The history is there. Go and read it. By not acknowledging history, Americans have always given themselves a way out of truly caring. As a kid, I saw social services take children away from their parents for the crime of being poor. Since America treats addiction like a crime, I've also seen my fair share of families destroyed by government agencies and the judicial system. Disenfranchised African American and Latinx children are ripped from struggling families and many times put into even more dangerous environments. Sure, some lives have been saved, but in too many cases children died.

Forgive me or don't, but I'm calling bullshit on fake outrage. When Melania Trump sauntered onto a plane to visit children held illegally at an immigration prison, she proudly wore an army-green coat that read I REALLY DON'T CARE. DO U? Her act remains not only immeasurably cruel and immensely stupid, but more importantly, telling. The whole administration spoke through that coat, and the villains asked us the most important question of all: Do you really care? They called our bluff. The billionaires' club bankrolling the Republican party and its racist agenda are showing us what they care about. They are using the influence money can buy to keep as many Americans racist, xenophobic, homophobic, Islamophobic, and averse to facts as possible. And ultimately, to keep all of us economically enslaved.

You might disagree with me; however, I don't believe we care enough. Sure, we responded to Melania Trump by blowing up social media with responses like "Yes, I care, bitch," and so on. But we are too caught up in surviving the rat race to do much more than that. At least, we believe we are. And we're afraid. A steady diet of police brutality videos combined with the nightly news has ensured that. In addition, average Americans, unwilling to accept the reality of their situation, are struggling to determine what their political capital looks like. We can't compete with the millions of dollars billionaires are pumping into politics (see *Citizens United*). In his 2014 *The Hill* article "Who Rules America?," Allan J. Lichtman reported:

> A shattering new study by two political science professors has found that ordinary Americans have virtually no impact whatsoever on the making of national policy in our country. The analysts found that rich individuals and business-controlled interest groups largely shape policy outcomes in the United States.

What can we do?

When news of the child separations went viral, thousands of people marched across the country. I was one of them. I stood in front of city hall with my wife and children in Newark, New Jersey, and we exercised our right to peaceful protest. We marched to the immigration building, people shouted, and people sang. One woman at the march held up a sign that read NO DEPORTATION WITHOUT REUNIFICATION. Undoubtedly, she missed the memo that the American government shouldn't mistreat or immediately deport asylum seekers. Especially when that very same American government created the instability that led to the refugees seeking asylum in America in the first place.

On that day, I realized that the only way to be heard was by getting out onto the streets. The larger a peaceful protest is, the more inconvenient it becomes to the power structure, and the more attention it gets. The visual representation of resistance emboldens others to find a way to resist. On that day, I remembered a picture I'd seen of the famous 1963 March on Washington. I wondered what it would look like if every city, in every state across America, organized an equivalent march to take place on the same day. What would it look like if we completely shut America down until our demands were met?

The oligarchy is waging an extremist economic war against us, and children are suffering the most. If you know history, then you know they are capable of so much worse: genocide, totalitarianism, torture, and more. There is no hero coming to save us. There is no hero coming to reunite all the scattered and suffering children with their desperately waiting parents. We must do it, all of us. The racists and sufferers of isms and phobias have found their heroes in the new Republican party. They've been conditioned by institutions to fall in line, to become what historian Timothy Snyder, in his book *On Tyranny: Twenty Lessons from the Twentieth Century*, calls people who "obey in advance" or who perform "anticipatory obedience." Snyder writes:

> Because enough people in both cases voluntarily extended their services to the new leaders, Nazis and communists alike realized that they could move quickly toward a full regime change. The first heedless acts of conformity could not then be reversed.

We've seen examples of this already. VICE News ran a segment on Trump supporters outside of Revolution Books in Berkeley. Not only did they threaten to burn down the bookstore, but one of them said, "Your genocide is coming!"

In his essay collection *Chronicles of a Liquid Society*, the late Italian writer Umberto Eco wrote of heroes:

> Brecht reminds us in his play *Galileo*: "Unhappy is the land that needs heroes." Why unhappy? Because it lacks people who do their duty honestly, responsibly, and "with professionalism." That's when a country searches desperately for a heroic figure, and awards medals left, right, and center. An unhappy land, then, is one whose citizens no longer know where duty lies, and seek a charismatic leader who tells them what to do. Which, if I remember correctly, is what Hitler promulgated in *Mein Kampf.*

Recently, I decided to confront a lifelong friend on his stance concerning the stolen children. I'll preface this by saying that he's a Seventh-day Adventist and that he voted for Trump twice, like many Catholics and members of other Christian denominations, because the Republican party is anti-abortion. I asked him point-blank what he thought about children being taken from their parents, being locked up far and wide, and with no plan for reuniting them. He responded that they shouldn't come here if they know that could happen. I rephrased the question: Shouldn't we treat children, their parents, and people in general with dignity? He looked me right in the face and said, "I'm a Republican and a Christian. What do you want me to say? I support my party and my faith." This man's parents are immigrants to America, one of them undocumented for a long time, and not even this fact prevented the entire clan from voting for Trump. That was but one more moment of affirmation for me that we're approaching critical mass. We're no longer operating as human beings centered on what's good for our humanity. Instead, we are upholding institutions even when they are driving us off a precipice.

Marvin Gaye's classic album *What's Going On?* is frighteningly relevant today. That the album's themes, topics, and concerns still apply is an indictment of us all. In "Save the Children," Gaye asks, "Who really cares? Who's willing to try?"

Who, indeed?

I Believe That We Will Win

Heading into the summer of 2014, I was psychologically exhausted. I'd survived a rough spring scraping by as an adjunct and working side hustles. In December 2013, the Republican Congress canceled the federal unemployment extension right before Christmas (ho, ho, ho). I had expected the spring to be rough. However, when all my summer classes were canceled due to low enrollment, things took a turn for the worse. Summer 2014 would be another tough season. My wife and I cut babysitting out of the budget, and I took on our childcare needs full time. I should have used the extra time to write, but for an avid sports fan, the ultimate distraction loomed ahead.

The World Cup was a couple weeks away! My wife's uncle slapped me on the back. "Sit around and watch the World Cup," he said. All the commercials I'd sleepwalked through of the American Outlaws chanting and hollering came flooding back. Our mantra, Team USA's battle cry, was "I believe that we will win! I believe that we will win!" What else could I do?

I sat back and watched all the Team USA documentaries, fanfare, and shenanigans. I got the kids into it, and my mother-in-law too. Whenever anything related to Team USA came on, we were on it. And when the World Cup started, I was in front of the television for every game. The USMNT (United States men's national soccer team) games were an event at my house. I couldn't sit down during the games. I watched each one standing inches from the television. I posted pictures of myself on Facebook. In some I sported my Clint Dempsey jersey, other pics were of game highlights, and some were of crowds of Team USA fans celebrating. And when Dempsey scored a goal against Ghana in the first minute of their first game, I was ready to write a collection of poems to commemorate it.

The US men's national soccer team became rock stars. The head coach, Jürgen Klinsmann, a legend of German *fútbol*, had infused the roster with a few American-born but foreign-raised players. It was a spin on the American immigrant story. The starting roster represented the ethnic smorgasbord many Americans see every day. Maybe our famous melting pot is why the world of fútbol harbors some anti-American sentiment. There's no homogeny and no centuries-old tradition on which to pin our fútbol aspirations. There's the desire to prove we belong. And ain't that America?

The underdog thing is a big reason why I root for American soccer. I'm a minority, an underdog, but I belong. I'm American. I can make it. I was all in. America, baby. America. "I believe that we will win."

*

You know the storyline, the one where the outcast makes her way into the upper crust and we're rooting for her, but we're also waiting for the crisis of conscience. We know it is coming because we know being a follower means giving away a very important part of oneself. In this kind of movie, our hearts plummet as we wonder what the hell she was thinking. I experienced the same crisis when I googled "Brazil, World Cup." The images alone—of women, children, and old people bludgeoned by police and kicked out of their homes to make room for the new stadiums—were horrific. There were protest marches, riots, and militarized police squads everywhere. During the height of my World Cup frenzy, I came crashing down.

I could no longer look at the massive crowds that gathered in parks, town squares, and bars to watch the USMNT play without feeling melancholy. I couldn't look in the mirror, nor could I perpetuate World Cup media hype on Facebook. I decided I would instead post articles, videos, and photos of the ongoing protests. I wanted to make sure they didn't go unseen, but I also wanted to feel I was a part of the protest. I know that compassion without action isn't enough and that there are difficult questions surrounding Facebook activism. It may not always constitute a moral act, but it is one small way to create visibility.

I felt solidarity for disenfranchised Brazilians and for their political and socioeconomic struggles because I'm familiar with them. My government overlooked my needs and the needs of countless Americans when they discontinued the federal extension of unemployment benefits. Edward Snowden's disclosure of government spying on American citizens revealed new civil rights violations every other day. The summer of 2014 kicked off an explosion of police violence against Black men and women not seen for decades, and never so publicly. New stories and cell phone videos of police killing or brutalizing Blacks, Latinxs, women, and Indigenous people popped up hourly.

The drafts of Walt Whitman–styled soccer poems I wrote quickly became kindling. Maybe I was desperate to escape the turmoil and find a distraction. I was spiritually and psychologically fatigued from my own struggles, and maybe the thousands of Americans blindly rooting for the group of young men on the fútbol pitch felt the same way. Perhaps we believed this team could bring us together. After all, the players were competing for respect, and it's not their fault that America is spiraling out of control. Maybe the battle cry "I believe that we will win," coined by the American Outlaws, the USMNT's supporters, has multiple layers that extend beyond the pitch. That might be too easy. Jorge Luis Borges, the legendary Argentinian writer and poet, famously said, "Nationalism only allows for affirmations, and every doctrine that discards doubt, negation, is a form of fanaticism and stupidity."

Borges hated the idea of a national fútbol team. I love sports, and reconciling that with alert and active citizenship is demanding and complex. Recently, a good friend and I spoke of the Roman Empire's bread and circuses: appease the poor with bread and entertain rich and poor alike with sports. Whether we acknowledge it or not, national teams play a huge role in political diversion.

* *

It is also critical to acknowledge that arguably the most fútbol-obsessed country in the world vehemently protested their national team and the biggest fútbol competition in the galaxy on home soil. This is Brazil we're talking about. Brazilians are practically born playing soccer, and outside the upper class and super rich who sipped the government Kool-Aid, no Brazilian wanted to spend the billions required to host the World Cup. Millions upon millions of dollars were poured into building new stadiums and renovating older venues. Meanwhile, countless Brazilians lack access to safe housing, affordable healthcare, well-paying jobs, and meaningful education.

Brazilians protested FIFA, fútbol's international ruling body, and the World Cup competition because compliance meant delving further into socioeconomic hell, and it still does. Years of economic disparity, neglect, and disenfranchisement had reached a boiling point. For far too many Americans, this story is all too familiar.

There I was, one with throngs of other Americans experiencing hardships similar to my Brazilian counterparts and acting like the blind nationalists Borges disdained. And in the home of fútbol, they immediately turned their backs on the game to fight for what matters. I can already hear your argument: "Sport transcends politics, race, etc. . . . These kinds of protest should remain outside of sport . . . Sport should be an escape from all of that."

Sports can transcend when given the opportunity. If the Brazilian national team had boycotted the World Cup and stood in solidarity with the underprivileged communities many of them came from, then yes, transcendence and solidarity could have happened. That would have been a great story. Go ahead and ask Muhammad Ali, Jim Brown, Kareem Abdul-Jabbar, Roberto Clemente, Tommie Smith, and John Carlos if civic discourse should be left out of sports. Pelé, arguably Brazil's greatest fútbol player, said, "It's clear that politically speaking, the money spent to build the stadiums was a lot, and in some cases was more than it should have been . . . Some of this money could have been invested in schools, in hospitals . . . Brazil needs it. That's clear."

* * *

I wish I could say that I boycotted the rest of the World Cup, but that would be a lie. The truth is I'm addicted. I am complicit. Currently, I'm awaiting the UEFA Champions League final, the Women's World Cup, and the NBA finals. I sit with hard questions as I wait and as I watch. Is there such a thing as innocent patriotism? No. Do I have to give up sports completely to go against the bread and circuses? Probably. It's too easy to become part of the dangerous narrative, the lie promoted by our media, corporations, politicians, and even certain educational institutions. The narrative encourages us to be oblivious to the struggles of others and to ignore them in the name of class and racial privilege. The narrative affirms that if the government is spying on us, it must have a good reason. It also affirms that if the police are indiscriminately killing citizens, then there must also be a "good" reason. No to all of this.

In his essay "Everybody's Protest Novel," James Baldwin writes:

> The aim has now become to reduce all Americans to the compulsive, bloodless dimensions of a guy named Joe . . . It must be remembered that the oppressed and the oppressor are bound together within the same society; they accept the same criteria, they share the same beliefs, they both alike depend on the same reality.

Written in 1949 as a response to *Uncle Tom's Cabin*, Baldwin's words are powerfully relevant to our social and political landscape to this day. Do we accept the reality we are living, what our eyes and experience tell us, or the reality we are fed by the media machine?

* * * *

At the end of that summer, I was hired for a full-time teaching position at a local community college. I am grateful. My family and I seem able to improve upon our middle-class life. I can spoil my kids, take vacations, and participate in a little conspicuous consumption. The neighborhood we live in is far from a favela, but fifteen to twenty minutes away are the neighborhoods I grew up in, and they are like favelas. It would be very easy for me to feel "taken care of" and to fall back into the crowd, to believe the narrative. I could forget the struggles in the hood, the countless adjuncts still scraping to make ends meet, and the disappearing middle class. I could forget the twelve stadiums going mostly unused in Brazil, even though a group of architects wants to turn them into housing for the poor and houseless. And I could ignore that FIFA walked away with at least two billion dollars.

FIFA became the subject of a massive investigation. Almost every high-level executive in the organization has been indicted for corruption and bribery, and its president at the time, Sepp Blatter, resigned. The messiness and complexity I'm wrestling with can't be resolved neatly in the world we live in, or in this essay. It's not entirely a contest of conscientiousness versus apathy either. Maybe it has something to do with the less comfortable question of what activism looks like today and how we go about actually doing good in this world. I want to enjoy sports, but I also want the world to be better for the people sports impact.

I want to believe that we, the writers who write about these issues; we, the hardworking people who pull ourselves up out of favelas all over the world; we, the people who are continually left behind; and we, the people who care enough to do something, anything, to bring others with us, will win. I'm going to keep trying the best I can. I believe that we will win.

Amiri Baraka

In Unity and Struggle

I miss Amiri Baraka. I miss his ferocity, his observations, and his powerful artistic expressiveness. I miss him tapping the side of the podium, keeping time to an imaginary metronome, improvising his own horn, or making sure the horn player (when there was one) was on time. I miss the faces of the young people in the crowd while Amiri Baraka was reading. How they marveled at the humor contained in his poetic truth, and the passion. I miss his ability to take oppositional views, his antagonism. I miss his contrarianism. In his introduction to *Somebody Blew Up America & Other Poems*, Kwame Dawes keenly observes the following:

> Baraka will tease us, toy with us, play with us, undermine us. He is the guy who stands on the playground teasing someone. We watch him and we find what he is saying funny because we always felt the same way about the guy he is teasing. So we think, "Hey, this guy is cool, let me join him." Yet, the moment we open our mouths to start to throw insults, he turns on us. He changes the game. Or sometimes, he takes it further, as if he is trying to test us, now, and not the person he is teasing. He goes so far and we are left bedlamized in the middle—not sure where we stand. We stand there dumbfounded. We feel betrayed, and he is grinning. We walk away

shaking our heads. This revolutionary figure does not offer us easy paths to the revolution.

There are no easy paths to revolution, and there are no all-knowing swamis either. Baraka didn't pretend to be one. He was smart enough to know that followers, or a following, are not a sign of truth. His tenacity challenged you, us, to question his motives, and by extension the motives of everyone around us. You need to know what you don't know, Jack. And what makes you think you know what you think you know?

*

Baraka's anger was as important to his work as it was to his delivery. Anger is sorely missing from poetry today. As a young man of Caribbean descent with African roots, living in a racially polarized America, I needed the anger I found in Baraka's poems. I still need anger at racial injustice, economic disparity, and willful ignorance. They helped me come to terms with my identity, and they allowed me to challenge the microaggressions around me head-on. On the last day of the 2014 Dodge Poetry Festival, there was a tribute to Amiri Baraka. Several well-known poets spoke about the impact of Baraka's work on their lives. Poet Natalie Diaz expressed that although she didn't know Baraka personally, his work gave her permission to be angry: "it allowed us to be warriors again." The epigraph to "Somebody Blew Up America" is a wise and articulated expression of the kind of anger I'm talking about: "All thinking people oppose terrorism. But one should not be used to cover the other."

Yet it seems that today's oppositional narrative wants to be more—I'm not sure what exactly—maybe nuanced, or sophisticated. Some of the blame for the lack of published angry poetry must go to the gatekeepers. Many writers and poets of color have stopped referring to editors as editors. The title of "gatekeepers" seems appropriate because they are gatekeeping entry to the world of publication. That the "big" houses would not publish an icon of American poetry like Amiri Baraka should tell you all you need to know. Baraka took notice: "When I was saying, 'White people go to hell,' I never had trouble finding a publisher. But when I was saying, 'Black and white, unite and fight, destroy capitalism,' then you suddenly get to be unreasonable."

In his essay "The Writing Class: On Privilege, the AWP Industrial Complex, and Why Poetry Doesn't Seem to Matter," Jaswinder Bolina writes:

> But poetry is supposed to be an art, which means it should at least attempt to represent the society in which it's produced. It can't fully do this if its primary mode of production inherently excludes large swaths of the population. The risk of such exclusions is that they limit the variety and appeal of the kind of writing produced in graduate programs. Nearly every complaint about contemporary poetry in the United States, whether in reference to the lack of diversity among those publishing it or to its opacity or to the very credibility of the genre itself, is rooted in this basic dynamic.

To take this a step further, poetry must also include its voices of discontent, if not feature them. However, the gatekeepers and the dominant mode of discourse, or what Erica Hunt calls "master narratives," determine agitation, instigation, antagonism, and contrarianism in literature today.

If Charles Bernstein had kept Erica Hunt's essential essay "Notes for an Oppositional Poetics" out of *The Politics of Poetic Form*, if Graywolf Press had kept out Claudia Rankine's *Citizen: An American Lyric*, if Agate Publishing had kept out Kiese Laymon's *How to Slowly Kill Yourself and Others in America*, the landscape for oppositional voices would be more of a wasteland than it already is. In stark contrast, Baraka founded Totem Press and self-published *Preface to a Twenty Volume Suicide Note*. Had self-publishing been the pariah it is today in the 1960s, America might have missed out on what is arguably its most intense love-hate relationship with a poet. The collection's titular poem is an intense meditation on isolation and despair that remains relevant and necessary to this day:

> Lately, I've become accustomed to the way
> The ground opens up and envelopes me
> Each time I go out to walk the dog.

Or the broad edged silly music the wind
Makes when I run for a bus . . .

Things have come to that.

And now, each night I count the stars.
And each night I get the same number.
And when they will not come to be counted,
I count the holes they leave.

Nobody sings anymore.

And then last night I tiptoed up
To my daughter's room and heard her
Talking to someone, and when I opened
The door, there was no one there . . .

Only she on her knees, peeking into

Her own clasped hands.

Baraka's brilliance lies in his ability to write "Preface" and also write
a poem like "S O S." The latter poem meditates on the singular ele-
ments of being while rallying Black people to overcome the struggle:

Calling black people
Calling all black people, man woman child
Wherever you are, calling you, urgent, come in
Black people, come in, wherever you are, urgent, calling
you, calling all black people
calling all black people, come in, black people, come
on in.

∗ ∗

As we lose our elders, we lose our connection to the old ways of
opposing and protesting power structures. Once upon a time, opposi-
tion or protest would see Baraka, James Baldwin, Gerald Stern, Maya

Angelou, Jack Agüeros, and others march in defiance, but today's poets have social media. In 2014, in the wake of Michael Brown's and Eric Garner's murders at the hands of police, protest marches sprung up all over the country, and it was via social media like Twitter and Facebook that America heard the *real* story—the one mainstream media couldn't cover objectively.

That same year, Grove Press released *S O S: Poems 1961–2013*, a collection of over fifty years of Baraka's poetry. There are some questionable interpretations of Baraka's work, and inconsistent versions of various poems in *S O S* (as observed by Aldon Lynn Nielsen on his blog *Heatstrings*). However, Baraka's work is now available in the "mainstream," and that has some benefits. Perhaps the winds are turning.

* * *

I think often of an event I attended at St. Mark's in NYC. Baraka was reading, and afterward I went up to him with a couple of his books and asked for his signature. He said, "How you doing, brother?" You know how when you're in front of someone you admire, and you're worried you might say the wrong thing? Well, that was me at that moment. I opened my mouth, and all I could say was a cliché thank-you. I said, "Thank you for being a voice I could trust, and even when I didn't always agree with you, I trusted your honesty."

There are some critics who still taint Baraka's legacy at every opportunity. They ignore all that he learned and the transformations he underwent as a writer and poet. These critics would dismiss the great body of work he's left behind. They'd denounce Baraka because of his early forays into antisemitism and homophobic language, all the while guarding T. S. Eliot's and Ezra Pound's places in the literary canon despite their own documented bigotry. Never mind that neither Eliot nor Pound attempted to establish their positions clearly on those issues the way Baraka did (see "Confessions of a Former Anti-Semite," the *Village Voice*). Baraka should be lauded for coming through them a better man, with his integrity and his honesty intact.

Amiri Baraka signed my book probably the same way he signed many others. But for me it's a hopeful omen. He wrote, "To Roberto, in Unity and Struggle."

The Self Sheltered in Place

On Pessoa, Heteronyms, and the Pandemic

We're all out of sorts at home. We don't know which hat we should be wearing: husband, dad, or professor; son, angsty teenager, or high school student trying to get by; corporate shark, wife, or mom, etc. As a society, we are afraid of death, anarchy, chaos, and the collapse of civilization at the slow hands of a plague, and that adds, however subconsciously or consciously, to our stress. As we shelter in place due to COVID-19, there's the haunting question of how well we know our own selves and those closest to us. Cabin fever pushes us toward the dark corners we don't normally have time to investigate.

Fernando Pessoa's poetry and his famous meditation *The Book of Disquiet* came to my mind as I sat at the dining room table, staring out the window, trying to tune out the noise in my house. Pessoa, a Portuguese poet and writer who lived from 1888 to 1935, utilized heteronyms (imaginary authorial characters created by writers to write in different styles). In his *New Yorker* article "Fernando Pessoa's Disappearing Act," Adam Kirsch opens by writing:

> If ever there was a writer in flight from his name, it was Fernando Pessoa. Pessoa is the Portuguese word for "person," and there is nothing he less wanted to be. Again and again, in both poetry and prose, Pessoa denied that he existed as any kind of distinctive individual. "I'm beginning to know myself. I don't exist," he writes in one poem. "I'm the gap

between what I'd like to be and what others have made of
me . . . That's me. Period."

Each of Pessoa's characters lives a completely independent life
from Pessoa and from the other characters he invented. His main
heteronyms are poets: Alberto Caeiro, a poet who questions nothing;
Ricardo Reis, a poet closer to Pessoa himself but who is a pagan living in a largely Catholic Portugal (Pessoa was critical of Portuguese
imperialism and colonialism); and Álvaro de Campos, yet another
poet, who believes in feeling everything intensely and in the artist's
need for isolation. For me, Pessoa's brilliance lies in acceptance. He
accepted all the voices in his head, soul, and heart and gave them
life on the page. Pessoa commanded these heteronyms in ways that
we cannot command our own selves. Perhaps that was his goal, to
isolate his essential nature by purging all his constructions. Carmela
Ciuraru, in her book *Nom de Plume: A (Secret) History of Pseudonyms*,
writes of Pessoa:

> It is crucial to make the distinction that Pessoa's "others"
> were heteronyms rather than pseudonyms. He insisted that
> they were separate from him. "I'm the empty stage where
> various actors act out various plays," he once wrote. In Pessoa
> country, unification was not possible or even desired. He was
> a breeder of beings, and always in pursuit of another. "I break
> my soul into pieces," he wrote, "and into different persons."

*

On some level, we all live as heteronyms. I can work myself into
this mode where I'm doing the poet-scholar thing—reading books
of criticism, literary theory, and meditations like Pessoa's, and envi-
sioning myself as some kind of Carl Phillips. At other times, I'm a
version of Amiri Baraka, an angry poetic consciousness full of love
for my people. At others, I'm Rimbaud—rake of a poet, drinking and
reveling—or I'm Neruda, falling in love repeatedly. I'm a dad, and a
college professor, and so on. These different versions of me are always
underneath the surface, always vying for position, and dominance.

Each one is a very real me, and I think hard about which one should dominate. My goal is to be the same me in front of my children that I am in front of my students, in front of my spouse, my mom, the blank page. I don't write, teach, or parent because of some attachment to how these personas should reward me. This is who I am, my nature.

And yet, we break ourselves into pieces. Like Pessoa, we create and re-create, adding onto and hiding selves away. On some level, Pessoa understood this and tried, by writing these heteronyms out, to learn more about them, about himself. Again, from Ciuraru: "[Pessoa] pretended relentlessly, employing more than seventy personae in his self-searching circus." This is like a technique sometimes used in therapy called externalization, where your therapist has you talk about one of your other selves to better understand that side of yourself. The goal is to speak to the constructs within you and to help you understand that part of yourself better, to differentiate that construct.

By comparison, we give our own little personages a certain number of hours a day, and then it's back in the box. The next day it's back to the routine, and on and on with the schism, the compartmentalization. For many, during this quarantine, we're enacting personas outside of their usual boxes: work, school, gym, church. We are seeing that there are possibilities, an existence where we don't need to be so fractured. As I read the passage below, I can identify with Pessoa's dilemma—the obsessing over my own selves, clashing with or embracing the selves in other people. My need for an essential oneness.

> I frequently do not recognize myself—it's something that often happens to people who know themselves . . . I accompany myself in the various disguises with which I am alive.

On occasion, I'm stopped cold by the version of me that appears at any given moment, or when he's not supposed to. I don't recognize me, but I know myself. And in those situations, I'm quiet. I accept what's happening and hide until another me, the right me, shows up. But what am I left with? Me(s), the versions of myself I know too well—paradoxical, confusing, and enlightening all at once. Perhaps the first-person narrative and the lyric speaker are an effort to corral these complex selves—to say we are one. Perhaps the goal of capitalism is a society of worker bees, bombarded on all sides by advertising and marketing that insist we are one simple thing: consumers. The "I" of those commercials speeding down a picturesque highway in a sleek sportscar, running determinedly on a treadmill in fresh kicks, wiping the kitchen counter down to a sparkle, etc. "You are one of these," capitalism tells you. That's it. Capitalism keeps the hamster wheel spinning; it tells us we are independent individuals while making us feel isolated. When I feel this way, I buy a new pair of sneakers. Maybe we spend our money frivolously to distract ourselves from that alienation. In *The Book of Disquiet*, Pessoa writes:

> Each of us is several, is many, is a profusion of selves. So that the self who disdains his surroundings is not the same as the self who suffers or takes joy in them. In the vast colony of our being there are many species of people who think and feel in different ways.

Maybe the danger lies in the attachments our heteronyms carry. These are attachments society saddles us with: expectation, ambition, gender, just to name a few. Or maybe the danger lies in what the Buddhists call delusion. We are slaves to attachment and delusion, and thus, we suffer. Some of us accept this fractured situation as a matter of course, others of us practice avoidance, and still others of us are oblivious. Ask yourself, what is your essential nature? Who are you really? Are you the empty stage, as Pessoa claimed, or are you the frantic production crew, trying to arrange it all? Pessoa also writes:

> Slavery is the only law of life, there is no other, because this law must be obeyed; there is no possible rebellion against it or refuge from it . . . The cowardly love we all have of freedom—which if it were given to us we would all repudiate as being too new and strange—is the irrefutable proof of how our slavery weighs upon us.

I believe we can break free from our chains—economic, psychological, and physical—but I also agree that we don't necessarily want freedom. It is comforting to have multiple heteronyms chasing carrots. It is scary to reject capitalism's indoctrination, career goals, family goals, material acquisitions, public respect, and social standing. True freedom scares us.

Fear is one reason so many Americans vote against their own best interests and resist lifesaving change. If the COVID-19 pandemic and the resulting lockdown teach us anything, it must be that we desperately need to create a more fluid and flexible labor environment, we need a better healthcare system, and we need to abandon capitalism ASAP. There are economic models out there that do not center wealth or the chasing of wealth. Unfortunately, it is far easier to exist as Alberto Caeiro, Pessoa's apathetic heteronym, described thus:

> He does not question anything whatsoever; he calmly accepts the world as it is . . . He is free of metaphysical entanglements. Central to his worldview is the idea that in the world around us, all is surface: things are precisely what they seem, there is no hidden meaning anywhere.

We don't all want the responsibility of freedom. Freedom is hard and requires sitting with yourself, stripped of embellishments—no structures, no constructions. Nothing exists in freedom but the emptiness of your essential nature, that empty stage. And just as important is having to do the hard work of actually seeing one another, seeing past the heteronyms and the masks, and in that way, liberating each other. I want to continue to be transformed—to be distilled into a oneness present under all circumstances, shattering all constructions and delusions, truly seeing. I want to be the opposite of the capitalist structure's illusion or delusion of oneness. I want a oneness of love and honesty. What a muddled and contradictory idea to even write. The COVID-19 pandemic is a nightmare, but if we could come out of it transformed . . .

"...a walk through this beautiful world..."

[On Bourdain and Suicide]

I am intimately familiar with suicide. In the past three years, I've lost a friend I loved dearly, a poet, to suicide. My cousin's son, who played with my own son in my backyard and was just eleven years old, took his own life. Before that, my sister took her own life. My daughter's best friend, a sixteen-year-old, took her own life. And in my turbulent youth, I, too, tried to take my own life. So let me disabuse you of thinking this essay is some form of celebrity worship. I know the reality, and I know the numbers.

Suicide Rates for Males and Females by Race/Ethnicity in the United States (2016)
Data Courtesy of CDC

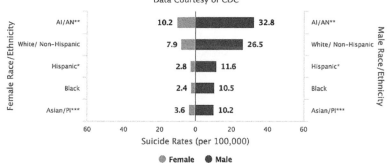

Suicide Rates (per 100,000)

● Female ● Male

*All other groups are non-Hispanic or Latino / **AI/AN = American Indian / Alaskan Native / ***PI = Pacific Islander

I also know that the biggest rate increase in American teen suicides is among Black and POC teenagers.

Teen suicide is soaring. The biggest rate increase was among black youth

Suicides per 100,000 10-to-17 year-olds
from 2008 to 2016:

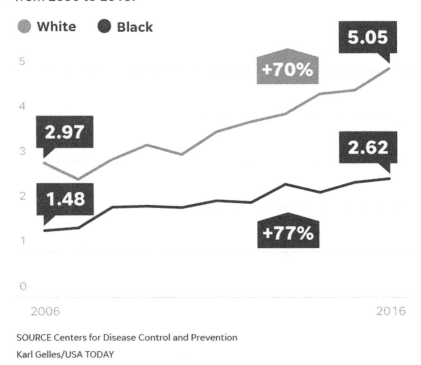

● White   ● Black

2.97

+70%

5.05

1.48

2.62

+77%

2006   2016

SOURCE Centers for Disease Control and Prevention
Karl Gelles/USA TODAY

When celebrities commit suicide or overdose on drugs, the media beats us over the head with insincere narratives. This eclipses the struggles of everyday people dealing with depression, drug addiction, and mental illness. And yet that doesn't mean we won't miss the musicians, writers, and other creative talents who used their gifts to bring us joy.

I want to talk to you about Bourdain and about suicide. I want to talk about it. To me, Anthony Bourdain wasn't really a celebrity. He lived as a traveler, a poet, and a malcontent with a desire to witness the unencumbered success of everyone looking to do good in the world. Bourdain, by his own admission a recovering addict, stated in an interview with *Fast Company* that he knew early on the difference between himself and those he described as addicts who saw no value in their lives. The difference, he claimed, was in his vanity. Somehow, when he looked in the mirror, he saw someone worth saving. He's that dude who pulls it together and leaves us in wonder. Because we know he's been to the knife's edge. We can see it in his eyes and hear it in his cynicism. Bourdain wasn't big on the idea of everybody being happy all the time, or content. He knew that couldn't be reality, and he gleefully bashed hipsters and gentrification for that very reason.

He handled *Parts Unknown* like an independent filmmaker creating a new film every week. He was a chef, and like me, he loved to cook for the people he loved. He was an everyman and one of us: us—that small percentage of the world (Black, white, whatever) that gets it. We understand that we're living in an oligarchy controlled by capitalism and that all the isms, phobias, religions, and economic systems are its control mechanisms. And because of this shared sensibility, I feel abandoned by Bourdain. I have some fucking nerve. I know. Believe me, I know. A man took his own life; a daughter, a mother, a lover, an ex-wife, and countless friends and fans survive him. And yet I feel abandoned. Like I lost a compatriot in the struggle.

I'll admit right now to something many of us minorities are guilty of: we love us some woke white folks. We're quick to "invite them to the cookout," as the saying goes. I suppose Bourdain is one of those woke white folks even though he hated being labeled as "woke." Shit, he'd probably do some of the cooking at the cookout. His privilege gave him a platform, and he used that platform to advocate for others as best he could. (There are limitations to white wokeness; we know this.) The dude went everywhere, sat down with anyone, and ate everything. Of Marseille, France, Bourdain wrote:

> A fair number of French will tell you in unguarded moments that "Marseille is not France," and what they mean by that is that it's too Arab, too Italian, too Corsican—too mixed up with foreignness to be truly and adequately French.
>
> But anybody who knows me knows that's exactly the kind of mixed-up gene pool I like to swim in and eat in. It is a

glorious stew of a city, smelling of Middle Eastern spices and garlic and saffron, and the sea.

On his pre–Hurricane Maria trip to Puerto Rico, at a dinner table surrounded by Boricuas committed to reclaiming their homeland, Bourdain and his guests discussed what's really going on between America and La Isla del Encanto. Bourdain asked:

> Why would a bank front seventy plus billion dollars into an economy that had been in decline for quite some time? Did they ever really have any reasonable expectation of getting their money back? Or was this just a cheap way of buying a country?

Bourdain's Puerto Rican hosts answer yes in unison. The singer-songwriter Alfonso "Tito" Auger emphatically rings an imaginary bell as if Bourdain had both asked and answered the million-dollar question.

Bourdain lived a life most people would envy, yet he fell into that number of white men who commit suicide. The hope, insight, and pleasure he presented to us on a weekly basis were not enough. Whatever kept me coming back every Sunday night, whatever got me through the week and took its place on the short list of things that bring me joy—my children, my career, poetry, and writing— whatever fuel he passed on to me and to his countless viewers by just being Anthony Bourdain was not enough. Therein lies the mystery of suicide. Another confession: I watch reruns of *Parts Unknown* trying to solve the mystery of why Anthony Bourdain killed himself. I comb the dialogue for anything cryptic. There are many moments in the show's final season, and there have been moments in his books. I think of a few passages from "The Rich Eat Differently Than You and Me," a chapter in his book *Medium Raw: A Bloody Valentine to the World of Food and the People Who Cook*:

> I was holed up in the Caribbean about midway through a really bad time. My first marriage had just ended and I was, to say the least, at loose ends.
> By "loose ends" I mean aimless and regularly suicidal . . .

The roads were notoriously badly maintained, twisting and poorly graded . . . And yet, every night I pushed myself to go faster and faster . . .

Here was the fun part: after making it past the more heavily trafficked roads of the Dutch side . . . I would follow the road until it began to twist alongside the cliff's edges approaching the French side. Here, I'd really step on the gas . . . For a second or two each night, for a distance of a few feet, I'd let my life hang in the balance, because, depending entirely on what song came on the radio next, I'd decide to either jerk the wheel at the appropriate moment, continuing, however recklessly, to careen homeward—or simply straighten the fucker out and shoot over the edge into the sea.

I audibly ask, "Anthony. Why bruh?" What a shitty thing to do on my part. The truth is, the pendulum swings, things change, and occasionally, we come out the other side. During the "Prime Cuts: Season Ten" episode of *Parts Unknown*, an episode which recaps all that season's travels, the director presents Bourdain with a question from a fan: "Is it worth it?" Bourdain answers:

I have a good life. I have the dream job. I have the best job in the world. There is a price to be paid when your dreams come true. Is it worth it? Yes. If it wasn't worth it, I wouldn't do it. So yes, I guess the answer is yes. It is worth it.

Once an episode, or once every few episodes, we get the camera shot of Anthony's back as he takes in a landscape: the Caribbean Sea in Puerto Rico, the Arabian Desert in Oman, the Si Phan Don in Laos. These are dramatic shots juxtaposing man with nature. On the surface, they present man in awe of the living world or simply enjoying it. Beneath the surface, the place where Bourdain always wanted to be, they are cinematic interpretations of literary themes, revealing, among other things, moments of loneliness. I wonder if Bourdain suffered from the overview effect. I first learned about the overview effect from a short film titled *Angelfish*. Author Frank White, in his book bearing the same name, coined the term:

The overview effect is a cognitive shift in awareness reported by some astronauts during spaceflight, often while viewing the Earth from orbit or from the lunar surface. It refers to the experience of seeing firsthand the reality of the Earth in space, which is immediately understood to be a tiny, fragile ball of life, "hanging in the void," shielded and nourished by a paper-thin atmosphere.

Sailors like Bernard Moitessier and countless explorers and mountain climbers also felt the effect. The realization that the world is so insignificant when compared to the cosmos, and that humanity is so fragile when compared to nature, is humbling. Realizing this over and over must be a staggering experience. Living with such a realization, when most of the world is consumed by its petty differences, must also be lonely.

It is paradoxical how easy it is to be lonely in a crowd, in the arms of your lover, in the presence of family and friends. There are people who hide it well. The reality is we're all lonely as fuck, because America is all about individualism. I think it was James Baldwin who said that American individualism makes you hate everybody in a quiet and desperate way. Bourdain had seen the other side. Many of the countries and American states he visited struggled with extreme poverty, inequality, and social problems. If his highs—dinner with chef Paul Bocuse, lunch with President Obama, getting inked by Japanese tattoo artist Takashi Matsuba—were as high as they looked to us, then the lows had to feel especially low. If you're susceptible to depression, this is a cruel pendulum.

*

The day my daughter's best friend died by suicide is seared into my brain. To protect her and her family's privacy, we'll call her Jane. The details of that day remain as clear to me as if it happened yesterday, as does the memory of Jane's face. It was overcast and humid. I was dropping my daughter off at a high school pep rally. I parked and walked my daughter up to the double doors to check everything out. Her friends were waiting for her, and they started to walk inside. I noticed Jane was far off, alone with her phone gripped tightly in both hands. I waved to her. She walked over. I asked her what was wrong. She said, "Nothing." She said it so casually, so don't-bother-me-dude-I'm-young-you're-old. And I understood that, but I pressed her anyway because I had this weird feeling in my gut. In the end, she said, "Nothing," and that was it. I let her walk away. It was mid-morning on a Saturday.

I drove to Essex County College in Newark to teach my Intro to Literature course. We read "Sonny's Blues" by James Baldwin. At the end of class one of my students began talking to me about family problems and how some of the dynamics in the story mirrored her own life. She spoke for an hour. I mostly just listened and offered encouragement where I could. We laughed, she cried, and afterward she expressed her gratitude to me for listening. "Don't think I didn't notice you hardly spoke," she said, and then added, "I appreciate you." I've been saying those very words to people ever since: "I appreciate you." The power of those simple words.

My biggest regret from that day is that I didn't take the energy from my talk with the student to follow up with Jane. Or maybe in the deepest parts of me, I regretted that Jane hadn't talked to me for an hour and felt better, and ultimately not killed herself. The universe gives us day-to-day life in weird ways like this. It gives—or, to be more accurate, shows—us hope and in the same breath drops steaming-hot reality in our laps. And the brink, that rubbery breaking point that appears unannounced every so often, isn't the danger we perceive it to be. It is not being jolted by the danger of the danger, not pulsing with the adrenalin, and not feeling much of anything that is deadly. When we enter that numbness, we are in the void.

**

Once upon a time I worked as assistant director of graduate admissions at a university. On a nondescript day the phone rang, and on the other end of the line—esther louise. No, that is not a typo. esther preferred her name be spelled in lowercase letters, and I'm going to honor that here, and always. She had a lot of questions about the Master of Fine Arts program in poetry, and I patiently answered each one. I was also a student in the program, so I was able to give her insider information. esther's most pressing question was, "Are you sure there's room for an old lady like me in your program?" I replied that I knew we had a place for her because I'd seen the student body. I'm so glad she believed me. She took to the program immediately. During her first semester, on the night of the student reading, when students were to present an original poem written during the residency, esther floored us with a poem about the dogwoods of her childhood in South Carolina and the love and teachings of her grandmother.

We became fast friends, going to readings together, exchanging poems, and sometimes, at those readings, sharing gossip about writers we did and didn't know. When she moved from Brooklyn to the Bronx, I went and lent a helping hand. In my eyes, I did what a friend should do—be present. Strangely enough, it was snowing off and on that day. Mild flurries, nothing major. esther spoke about the gentrification encroaching on the neighborhood: "But," knowing that I'm Dominican, she said, "there's a Dominican restaurant up the street and around the corner." Although she didn't hold too much with the menu, she treated me to stewed goat with rice and red beans. We continued our friendship and would continue it, I thought, for many more years.

I'm terrible at math, but I love to hear experts argue about the role of time in the universe. I see time as a constant, meaning that it is what it is. However, when we get caught up with living our lives, time becomes a whip-bearing taskmaster. It is then that time closes in around us, making us feel claustrophobic and harried. Time can isolate us in the void, disconnecting us from what's important. If we're not careful, the way we perceive what's happening in our lives, in relation to the way we perceive the time we have to deal with it, can disconnect us from normal existence.

The way we think about time in our daily lives can deceive us into losing touch with beloved friends. I lost touch with esther for almost three months. I'd been juggling projects, and one day I read one of esther's status updates on Facebook. The mood emoji expressed "feeling optimistic." It hit me that at that point in time, I did not know what was going on in my friend's life, what she might need from me, if anything, and if I was able to help. I resolved to call her and make sure she was okay. In the meantime, I replied to her Facebook post. A few days went by, and I hadn't called. Thinking back now, I'm sure the illusory phrase "I'm too busy" flashed through my mind. Then I received a phone call. I can't remember now who it was, but the person on the other end of the line told me that esther louise had taken her own life. Here arose another shock, another trauma, and another ripple in my soul.

Experts claim you can't go backward in time; at least, not yet. That fact, however, doesn't prevent me from wishing I could go back and make that phone call.

* * *

I was texting and emailing back and forth with my friend Ann about Bourdain's suicide. That night I dreamt I was in a Brazilian jiujitsu dojo. The dojo was crowded, and people sat or walked around, some wearing a *gi* (a martial arts uniform) and others in T-shirts and shorts. I had no idea what they were doing, but I knew they weren't training. For whatever reason, I was hemming and hawing over whether I could attend classes three nights a week. (In the waking world, I'm a Japanese jiujitsu practitioner.) A man gave me a white gi and white belt and then led me up some stairs to a mat. Anthony Bourdain was waiting for me on the mat, and we "rolled." Rolling is the practice of wrestling for position and submission in Brazilian jiujitsu. It looks like two people aggressively "hugging it out" on the floor, but it is an intense physical chess match with one person trying to make the other submit.

Bourdain was a solid blue belt in Brazilian jiujitsu. It is important to note that it takes about two years to earn a blue belt. He came in first place at the 2016 New York Spring International Open IBJJF Jiu-Jitsu Championship. You can imagine my surprise then when I put him in a leg lock, and he tapped out (I mean, it was a dream). My face felt hot. Part of me was embarrassed I won. We hugged and clasped hands. He looked me dead in the eyes, said, "My spirit's not right," and walked away. I woke up thinking about that Hanoi episode, when Bourdain sat down to lunch with President Obama. At the end of the meal, he asked the question on everyone's mind. Trump was escalating his campaign rhetoric and spewing a new and more shocking statement every day. President Obama sat there, in his characteristically open and hopeful manner. Bourdain asked: "Is everything going to be okay?"

* * * *

My plan seemed flawless. In my mind, I pictured everyone who claimed to love me crying, miserable, and full of remorse. I chose the most beautiful place in the ghetto I called home: a large park with trees, basketball courts and soccer fields, picnic areas, and bright stadium lights. The park, situated a few blocks from the housing projects, always had people coming and going. Eventually someone would stumble on my lifeless body, and the Shakespearian tragedy I'd plotted would be set in motion. It was textbook suicidal ideation.

Snow fell softly that evening. I stood in front of the bathroom mirror and swallowed four bottles of pills. I didn't even look to see what I was swallowing. After, I looked around the apartment, peeked my head into my mother's and then my sister's bedrooms. No one acknowledged or noticed me, and I took this as a slight, as justification for my actions. I quietly walked out, went to the park, and lay down on a park bench. As snow flurries landed all around me, I opened my mouth to catch them. Sleep crept in from the edges. Snowflakes slid down my throat like the pills I'd swallowed. I regretted my decision. In my haze, I thought to pray, so I did. Somehow, I woke up at my mother's front door, my sister slapping me in the face and trying to get me up from my knees. During the recovery I couldn't remember what I'd prayed for, only that the words "never again" featured prominently.

* * * * *

The art of lingering over the table after a meal and spending time together is called *sobremesa*. This beautiful activity can consist of solving the world's problems over after-dinner drinks, or it can also be something as simple as quietly enjoying fullness together. Bourdain invited viewers to countless meals and countless moments of sobremesa. In the Hong Kong episode, his meal with photographer Simon Go is priceless. Go is chronicling the disappearance of Hong Kong's independent shops, and he reminisces about dumpling, a thick piece of bread slathered in butter and deep-fried in a pan. Go's mother used to make it for him as a boy. When his mother and grandmother passed away, the dish died with them—until one day, when his aunt attempted to make it for him. One taste brought tears to his eyes, and the memories came flooding back. In describing this moment, Go became visibly emotional, and his eyes welled up with tears. That's sobremesa, and *Parts Unknown*.

Bourdain's virtuosity exists in presenting to us, as is, what food means to people and how it makes us all human. The opening and closing scenes of that same episode are haunting: Bourdain sitting alone, meditative, and writing in his notebook. Again, there's the classic *Parts Unknown* solo shot. We could read Bourdain's monologue as a confession of love for Asia Argento, but as is often the case with Bourdain, he juxtaposes this confession with a brutal truth:

> Chapter 1: To fall in love with Asia is one thing. To fall in love in Asia is another. Both have happened to me. The star ferry to Kowloon at night, the lights of Hong Kong behind me, it's a gift, a dream, a curse. The best thing, the happiest thing, yet also the loneliest thing in the world.

At the end of the episode, he walks through a crowd; they're on their phones recording the mélange of colors that is Hong Kong's skyline at night. The people are looking up at the grand image on their phones, as if the skyline in front of them was being broadcast from somewhere far away. This closing scene, a poetic expression, captures what twenty-first-century loneliness looks like. But somehow, some way, we must keep living.

Choosing a favorite episode of *Parts Unknown* is almost impossible. If I had to list a possibility, "Japan with Masa," is up there. The epigraph, spoken in Japanese, is an ars poetica on the restless creative spirit.

> I think I need more momentum. Power. That's why I'm creating all the time. I have a little bit of a crazy side. That's why I keep moving. I keep doing something. I can't sit still in the same place. I have to move. And still, I am learning.

Again, on the surface, the words are representative of Bourdain's spirit, as I know it from his show, his interviews, and his books. However, the lyrics from the *Parts Unknown* theme song express Bourdain's cynicism and his eye for brutal realism.

> I took a walk through this beautiful world
> I felt the rain on my shoulders
> I took a walk through this beautiful world
> I felt the rain getting colder

If you are in crisis, please call, text, or chat with the Suicide and Crisis Lifeline at 988, or contact the Crisis Text Line by texting TALK to 741741. If you are located outside the United States, call your local emergency line immediately.

ACKNOWLEDGMENTS

Thank you.

Bismillāhi raḥmāni raḥīm—All gratitude and reverence to the almighty God, the Most Gracious, the Most Merciful.

All gratitude and reverence to the ancestors, *ashé*! I am because of you, descended from Africans, and mighty.

To Ann, Darla, and Lynne—endless gratitude, always. And to Ysabel, for saying "You should try writing essays." Bless you. Here we are.

To everyone in the struggle. Every. One. Never let them steal your tongue. Speak. Write. Fight. Do not give oppressors the satisfaction of your silence.

For the Dominican Republic, Haiti, Africa, and Palestine.

Mad love.

*

I am grateful to the editors of the following publications, where these essays first appeared, sometimes in different versions.

English Kills Review: "Trapped in History"

Entropy: "I Believe That We Will Win" and "On Junot Díaz and the Literati"

Gawker: "black / Maybe," a version of which was then titled "Hiding Black Behind the Ears: On Dominicans, Blackness, and Haitians"

Huellas Literary Magazine: "'I Am the Darker Brother': On Michèle Stephenson's *Stateless* and Dominican Racism"

The New Engagement: "Traveling Freely"

Queen Mob's Teahouse: "Save the Babies"

The Root: "So, You're Afro-Latinx. Now What?"

Seven Scribes: "Home: An Irrevocable Condition"

Those People: "Ten Minutes of Terror"

An abbreviated version of "'I Am the Darker Brother': On Michèle Stephenson's *Stateless* and Dominican Racism" appeared on the North American Congress on Latin America (NACLA) website.

"Ten Minutes of Terror" also appears in the poetry collection *[Elegies]* (Flower Song Press, 2020).

"Home: An Irrevocable Condition" and "black / Maybe" also appear in the poetry collection *black / Maybe: An Afro Lyric* (Willow Books, 2018).

WORKS CITED

Ariel, Amani. "11 Must-Read Books That Center Powerful Afro-Latin@ Narratives." *Blavity*, September 30, 2015. https://blavity .com/11-must-read-books-that-center-powerful-afrolatin-narratives.

Baker, Jennifer. "First Diversity Baseline Survey Illustrates How Much Publishing Lacks Diversity." *Forbes*, January 26, 2016. https://www.forbes.com/sites/jenniferbaker/2016/01/26/first -publishing-diversity-baseline-survey/?sh=2e0f39c34159.

Baldwin, James. "A Conversation with James Baldwin." From "Perspectives: Negro and the American Promise" by National Educational Television, June 24, 1963. http://americanarchive.org /catalog/cpb-aacip-15-0v89g5gf5r.

Balko, Radley. "'Do Not Resist': A Chilling Look at the Normalization of Warrior Cops." *Washington Post*, September 30, 2016. https://www.washingtonpost.com/news/the-watch/wp/2016/09 /30/do-not-resist-a-chilling-look-at-the-normalization-of-warrior -cops/.

Baraka, Amiri. "Preface to a Twenty Volume Suicide Note" and "S O S." In *S O S: Poems 1961–2013*, by Amiri Baraka. New York: Grove Press, 2016.

Barker, Chris. Interview by Ilia Calderón. *CNN*, August 22, 2017. https://www.cnn.com/videos/cnnmoney/2017/08/22/univision -kkk-interview-cnnmoney.cnnmoney.

Bolina, Jaswinder. "The Writing Class: On Privilege, the AWP-Industrial Complex, and Why Poetry Doesn't Seem to Matter." Poetry Foundation, November 14, 2014. https://www.poetryfoundation.org/articles/70181/the-writing-class.

Bourdain, Anthony. "Bourdain's Field Notes: Marseilles." Explore Parts Unknown, September 25, 2017. https://explorepartsunknown.com/marseille/bourdains-take-marseille/.

Bourdain, Anthony. "Hanoi," "Japan with Masa," "Prime Cuts Season Ten," and "Hong Kong." *Anthony Bourdain: Parts Unknown*, 2013–2018.

Bourdain, Anthony. *Medium Raw: A Bloody Valentine to the World of Food and the People Who Cook.* New York: Ecco, 2010.

Burgess, Tamika. "10 Afro-Latina Authors You Should Know." *Ain't I a Latina?*, May 30, 2016. http://aintilatina.com/2016/05/30/10-afro-latina-authors-know/2/.

Castel, Raúl Zecca. "Extorted and Exploited: Haitian Labourers on Dominican Sugar Plantations." *openDemocracy*, September 14, 2017. https://www.opendemocracy.net/en/beyond-trafficking-and-slavery/extorted-and-exploited-haitian-labourers-on-dominican-sugar-plantati/.

Chen, Ken. "Authenticity Obsession, or Conceptualism as Minstrel Show." *Margins*, June 11, 2015. https://aaww.org/authenticity-obsession/.

Ciuraru, Carmela. *Nom de Plume: A (Secret) History of Pseudonyms.* New York: HarperCollins, 2011.

Civil Rights Digital Archive. Digital Library of Georgia, University of Georgia Libraries. https://crdl.usg.edu/.

Clement, Scott. "Millennials Are Just about as Racist as Their Parents." *Washington Post*, April 7, 2015. https://www.washingtonpost.com/news/wonk/wp/2015/04/07/white-millennials-are-just-about-as-racist-as-their-parents/.

Coates, Ta-Nehisi. *Between the World and Me.* New York: Spiegel & Grau, 2015.

Constitute Project. "Dominican Republic's Constitution of 2015." Constitute Project, 2015. https://www.constituteproject.org /constitution/Dominican_Republic_2015.pdf.

Cottrol, Robert J. "Coming into Their Own? The Afro-Latin Struggle for Equality and Recognition." *Grassroots Development* 28, no. 1, 2007. https://www.iaf.gov/content/publication/grassroots -development-focus-african-descendants-and-development/.

Dawes, Kwame. Introduction to *Somebody Blew Up America & Other Poems,* by Amiri Baraka. St. Martin, Caribbean: House of Nehesi, 2007.

Dove, Rita. "Parsley." In *Museum,* by Rita Dove. Pittsburgh: Carnegie Mellon University Press, 1983.

Eco, Umberto. *Chronicles of a Liquid Society.* Translated by Richard Dixon. Boston: Houghton Mifflin Harcourt, 2017.

Fernández, Tomás Robaina. "Essay: Why It Is Necessary That All Afro-Descendants of Latin America, the Caribbean and North American Know Each Other More." PBS. https://www.pbs.org /wnet/black-in-latin-america/essays/essay-why-it-is-necessary-that -all-afro-descendants-of-latin-america-the-caribbean-and-north -american-know-each-other-more/163/.

Figueroa, Jose. "Afro-Latinxs: Representation Matters." *Geeks of Color,* April 21, 2017. https://geeksofcolor.co/2017/04/21/afro -latinxs-representation-matters/.

Foley, Elise. "Deportation Separated Thousands of U.S.-Born Children from Parents in 2013." *HuffPost,* June 25, 2014. https://www .huffpost.com/entry/parents-deportation_n_5531552.

García-Peña, Lorgia. *The Borders of Dominicanidad: Race, Nation, and Archives of Contradiction.* Durham: Duke University Press, 2016.

Gaston, Herron Keyon. "Who Benefited from the Civil Rights Movement?" *HuffPost,* February 9, 2015. https://www.huffpost .com/entry/who-benefited-from-the-ci_b_6637798#:~:text= The%20movement%20didn't%20just,all%20marginalized %20groups%20and%20individuals.

Hicok, Bob. "The Promise of American Poetry." *Utne*, July 9, 2019. https://www.utne.com/arts/new-american-poetry-zm0z19uzhoe/.

Jaschik, Scott. "They Aren't Retiring." *Inside Higher Ed*, August 1, 2013. https://www.insidehighered.com/news/2013/08/02/new -study-shows-difficulty-encouraging-professors-retire.

Kanaar, Michelle. "Dominican Republic: The Haitian Sugar Work- ers Denied Their Pensions." *Equal Times*, December 16, 2015. https://www.equaltimes.org/dominican-republic-the-haitian?lang= en#.YD5eApNKho4.

Kirsch, Adam. "Fernando Pessoa's Disappearing Act." *New Yorker*, August 28, 2017. https://www.newyorker.com/magazine/2017/09 /04/fernando-pessoas-disappearing-act.

Levin, Abigail, and Lisa Guenther. "White 'Power' and the Fear of Replacement." *New York Times*, August 28, 2017. https://www .nytimes.com/2017/08/28/opinion/white-power-and-the-fear-of -replacement.html.

Lichtman, Allan J. "Who Rules America?" *The Hill*, August 21, 2014. https://thehill.com/blogs/pundits-blog/civil-rights/214857-who -rules-america/.

Lopez, Alan Pelaez. "An Open Letter to Afro-Latinxs: You Are Enough and It's Okay to Have Questions." *Everyday Feminism*, September 14, 2016. https://everydayfeminism.com/2016/09/open -letter-to-afro-latinxs/.

Masciotra, David. "The Punisher Skull: Unofficial Logo of the White American Death Cult." *Salon*, April 28, 2019. https://www.salon .com/2019/04/28/the-punisher-skull-unofficial-logo-of-the-white -american-death-cult/.

Minority Rights Group International. *Our Lives in Transit* (FULL). YouTube, April 20, 2017. https://www.youtube.com/watch?v= DAqGuj8AT1U.

Montilla, Yesenia. "The Day I Realized We Were Black." In *The Pink Box*, by Yesenia Montilla. Detroit: Aquarius/Willow Books, 2015.

Nunes, Andréa. "Life in the Dominican Republic's Sugar Fields: Resistance from the Bateyes." *Journal of Pedagogy, Pluralism, and Practice* 8, no. 1, 2016. https://digitalcommons.lesley.edu/cgi /viewcontent.cgi?article=1049&context=jppp.

Orloff, Judith. "The Health Benefits of Tears: Learn How Tears Can Benefit You and Improve Your Health." *Psychology Today*, July 27, 2010. https://www.psychologytoday.com/us/blog/emotional -freedom/201007/the-health-benefits-tears?eml.

PBS. *Black in Latin America*. PBS. https://www.pbs.org/wnet/black -in-latin-america/.

Pessoa, Fernando. "Introducing Alberto Caeiro." In *Poems of Fernando Pessoa*. Translated by Edwin Honig and Susan Brown. San Francisco: City Lights Books, 1998.

Public Justice Center. *Justice Diverted: How Renters Are Processed in the Baltimore City Rent Court*. Public Justice Center, December 2015. https://publicjustice.org/wp-content/uploads/2019/09 /JUSTICE_DIVERTED_PJC_DEC15.pdf.

Sherman, Natalie. "BDC Moves Forward 535 Million Port Covington TIF." *Baltimore Sun*, March 24, 2016. https://www.baltimoresun .com/2016/03/24/bdc-moves-forward-535-million-port-covington -tif/.

Snyder, Timothy. *On Tyranny: Twenty Lessons from the Twentieth Century*. New York: Tim Duggan Books, 2017.

Stephenson, Michèle, dir. *Stateless* (documentary). 2020.

Story, Louise. "As Companies Seek Tax Deals, Governments Pay High Price." *New York Times*, December 1, 2012. https://www.nytimes.com /2012/12/02/us/how-local-taxpayers-bankroll-corporations.html.

TeachThought. "25 of the Most Important Books about Racism and Being Black in America." TeachThought, March 23, 2017. https:// www.teachthought.com/education/books-about-racism/.

Watkins, D. *The Beast Side: Living and Dying While Black in America*. New York: Hot Books, 2016.

Zhang, Jenny. "They Pretend to Be Us While Pretending We Don't Exist." *BuzzFeed*, September 11, 2015. https://www.buzzfeed.com /jennybagel/they-pretend-to-be-us-while-pretending-we-dont-exist.

SOURCES

All possible care has been taken to trace ownership and secure permission for copyrighted material reproduced in this book. The author wishes to thank the following publishers and copyright holders. This page constitutes a continuation of the copyright page.

James Baldwin. "The Fire Next Time," "Encounter on the Seine: Black Meets Brown," "Stranger in the Village," and "Everybody's Protest Novel." From *The Price of the Ticket: Collecting Non-Fiction 1948 to 1985*, by James Baldwin. Copyright © 1985 by James Baldwin. Reprinted by permission of Beacon Press.

James Baldwin. "Death is easy (for Jefe)." From *Jimmy's Blues and Other Poems*, by James Baldwin. Copyright © 1983, 1985 by James Baldwin. Reprinted by permission of Beacon Press.

James Baldwin. "The Last Interview" © 1987 by Quincy Troupe. From *James Baldwin: The Last Interview and Other Conversations*. Copyright © 2014 by Melville House Publishing. Used by permission of Quincy Troupe and Melville House.

Audre Lorde. "Uses of the Erotic" and "Poetry Is Not a Luxury." From *Sister Outsider*, by Audre Lorde (Crossing Press/Penguin Random House). Copyright © 1984, 2007 by Audre Lorde. All quotes used by permission of the Charlotte Sheedy Literary Agency.

Willie Perdomo. "Nigger-Reecan Blues." From *Where a Nickel Costs a Dime*, by Willie Perdomo. Copyright © 1996 by Willie Perdomo. Used by permission of W. W. Norton & Company.

Fernando Pessoa. From *The Book of Disquiet*, translated by Margaret Jull Costa. Translation copyright © 1991 by Serpent's Tail, an imprint of Profile Books. Reprinted by permission of Profile Books.

Claudia Rankine. Excerpt from ["Hennessy Youngman aka Jayson Musson"], from *Citizen: An American Lyric*, by Claudia Rankine. Copyright © 2014 by Claudia Rankine. Reprinted by permission of the Permissions Company LLC, on behalf of Graywolf Press.

2015 Diversity Baseline Survey. Text copyright © 2015 by Lee & Low Books. Permission arranged with Lee & Low Books. All rights reserved. Learn more at www.leeandlow.com/about-us/the-diversity-baseline-survey.